Valentine : Coloring book

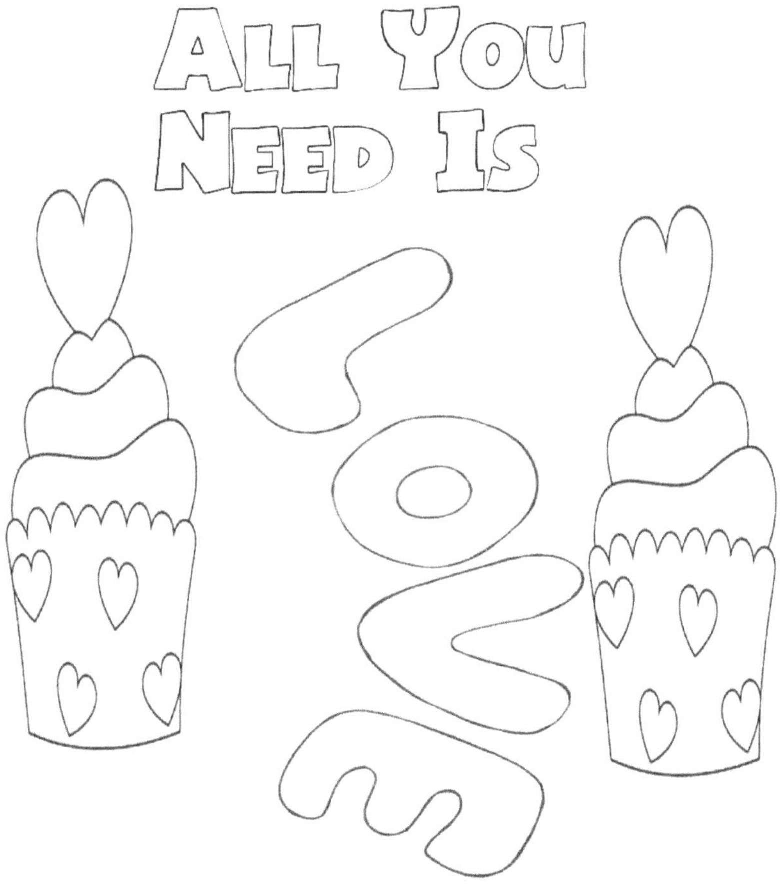

Nina Packer

All You Need Is LOVE: Coloring book For Kids

Published December 2017

ISBN-13: 978-1981764754

ISBN-10: 1981764755

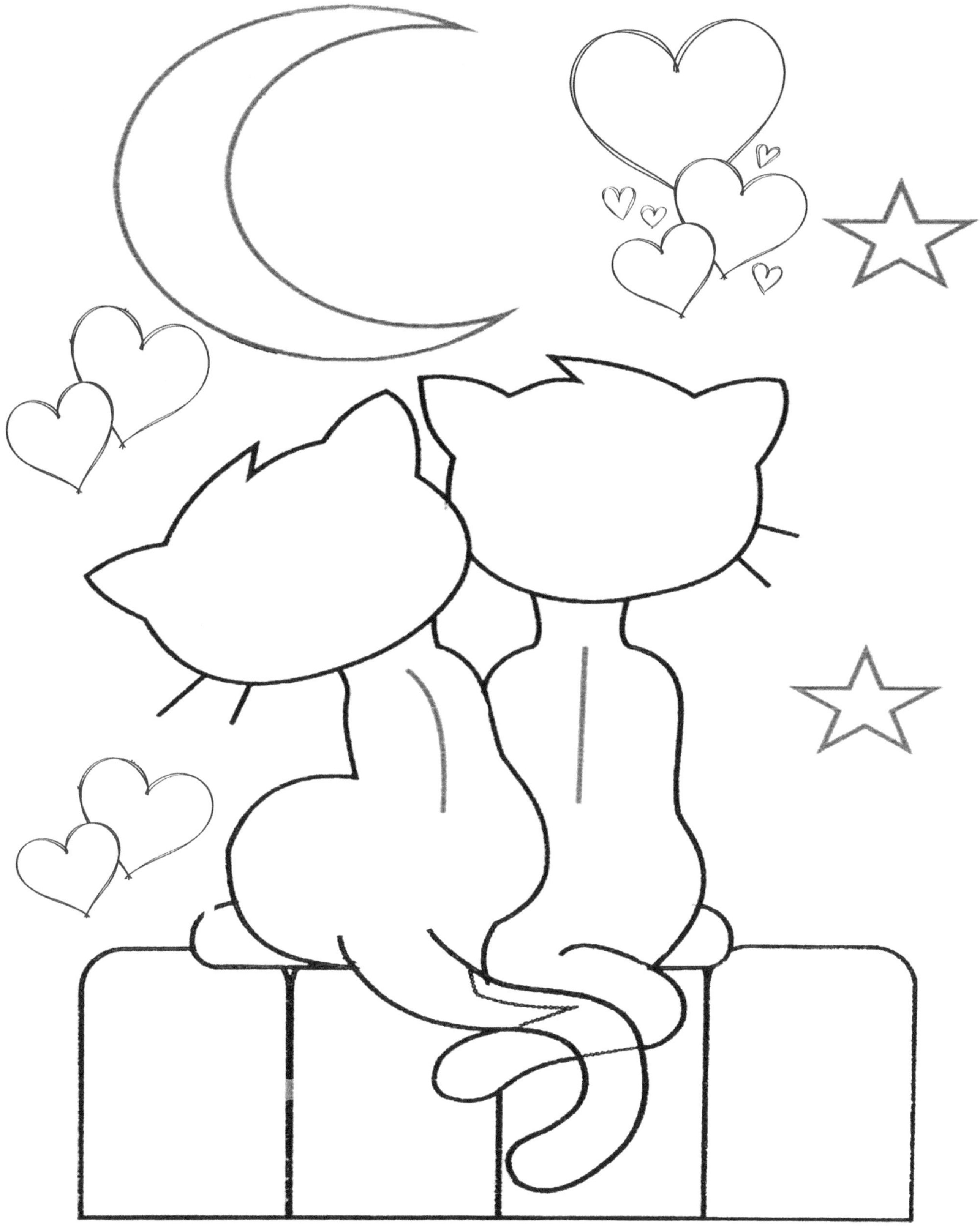

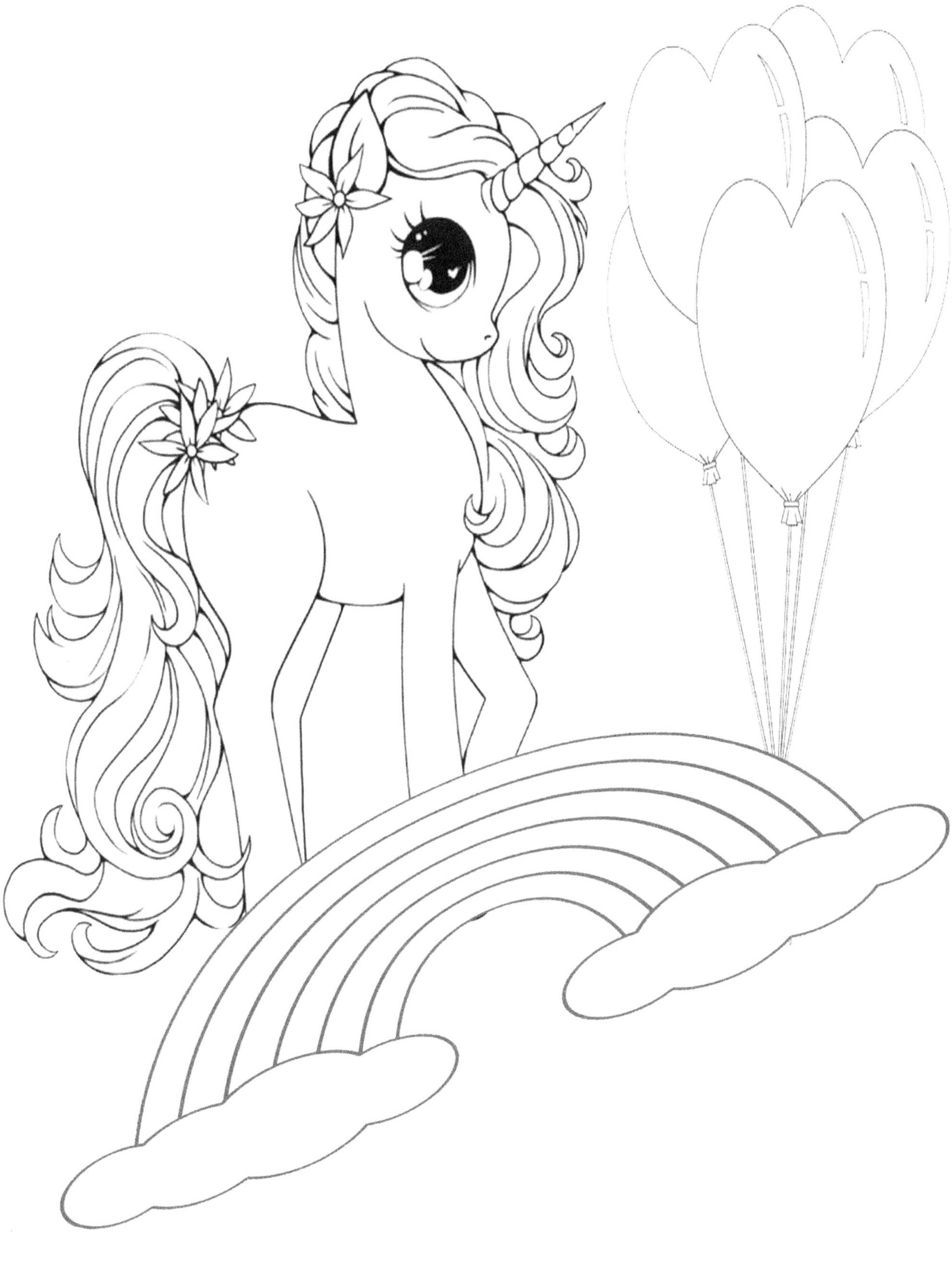

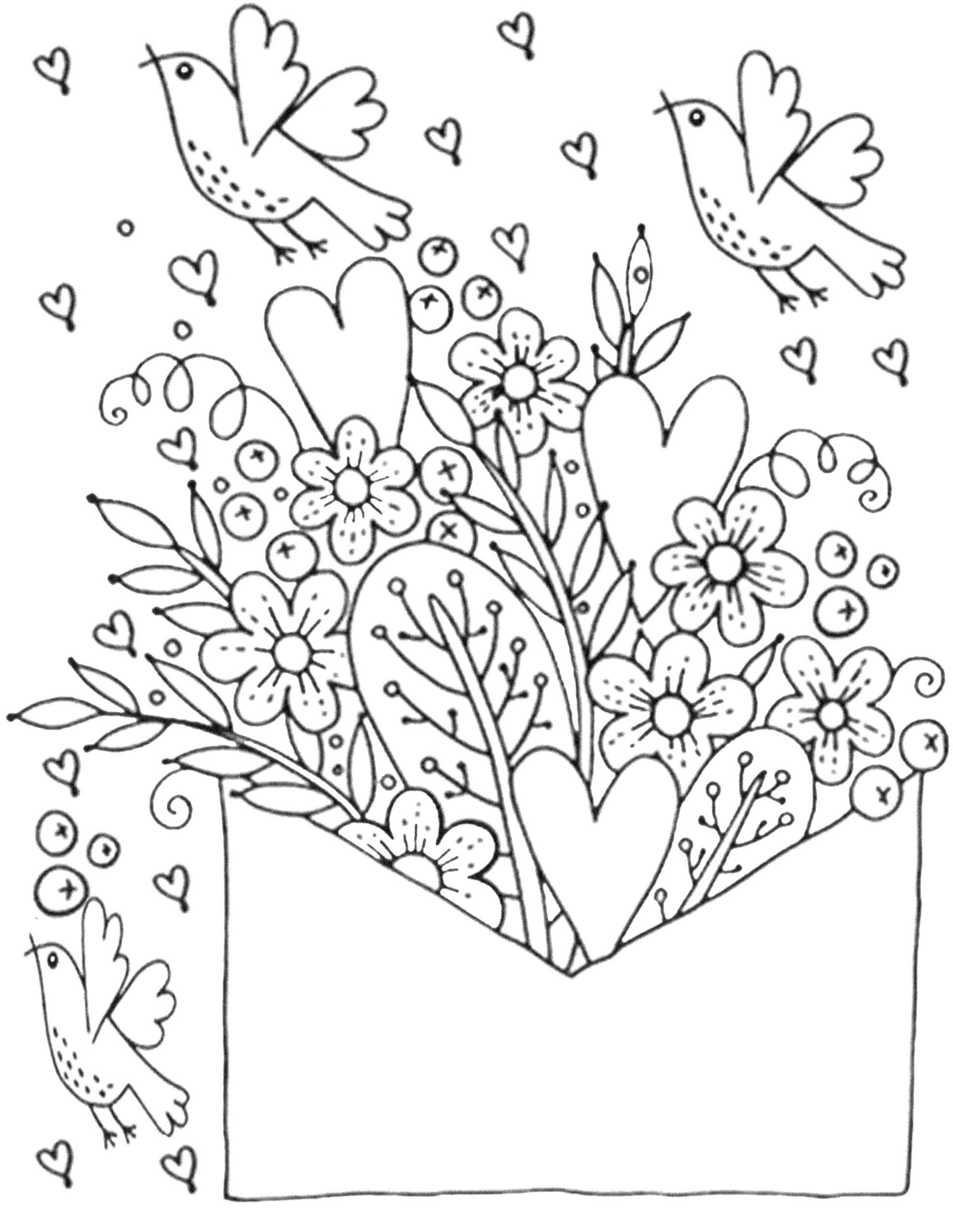

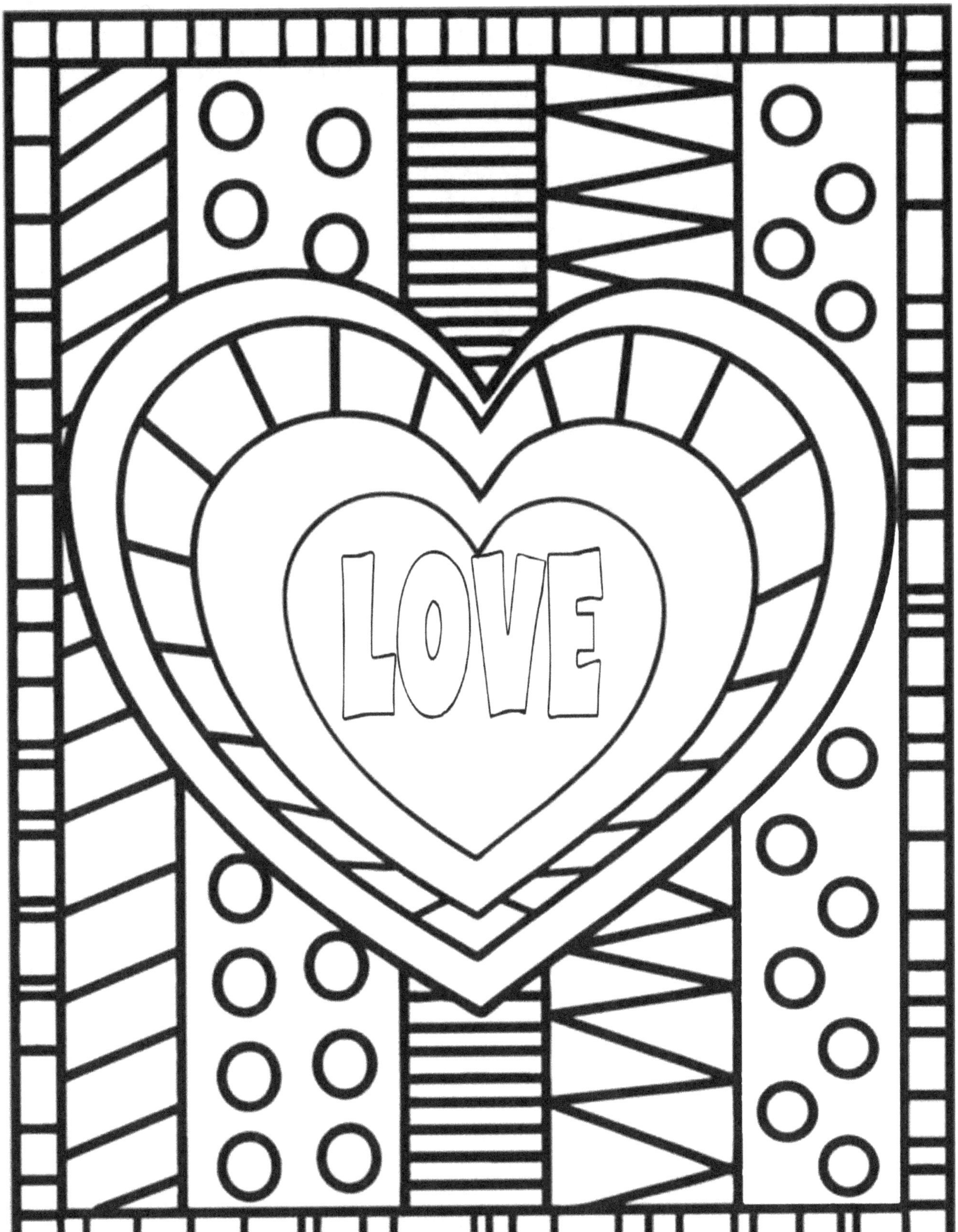
LOVE

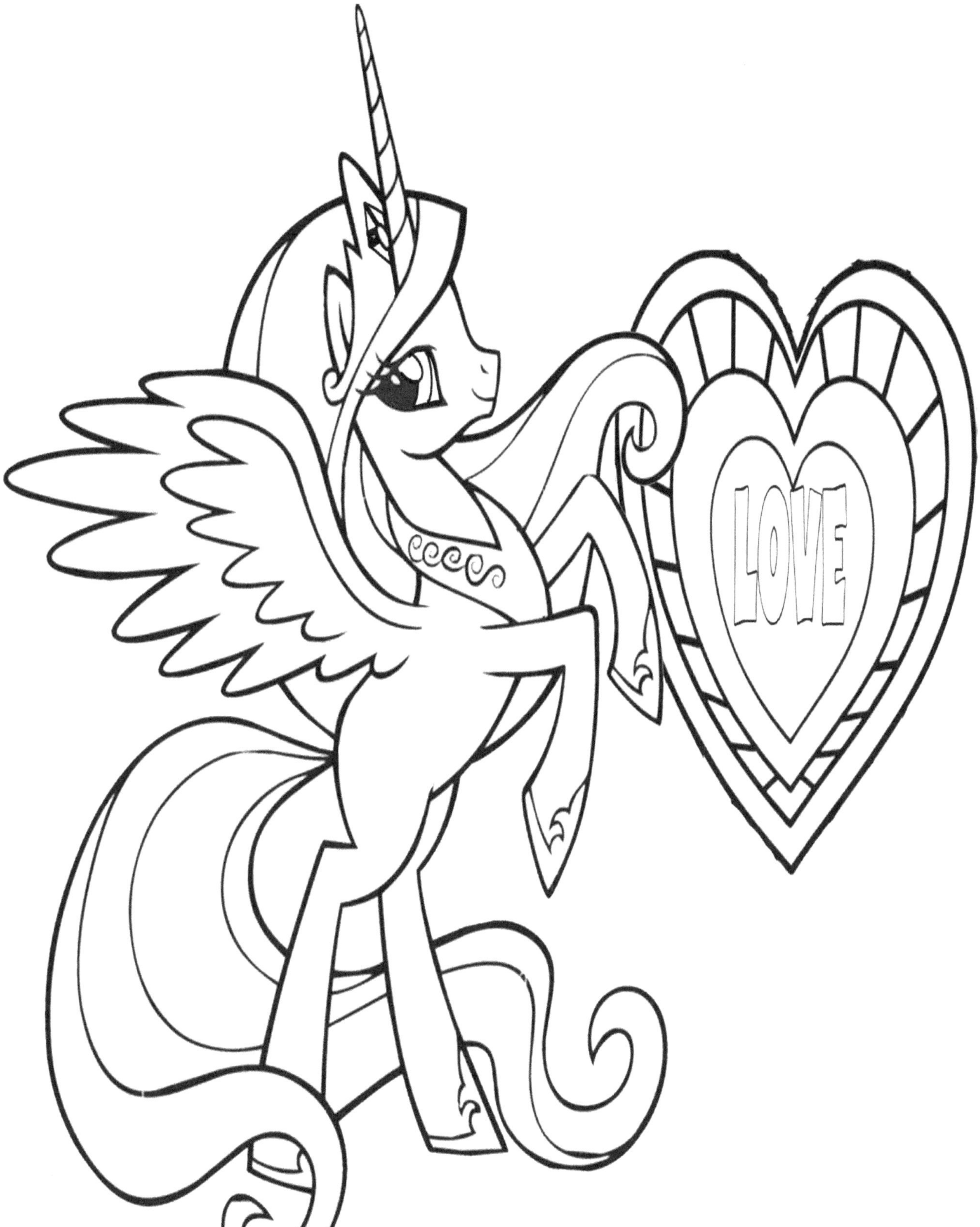
LOVE

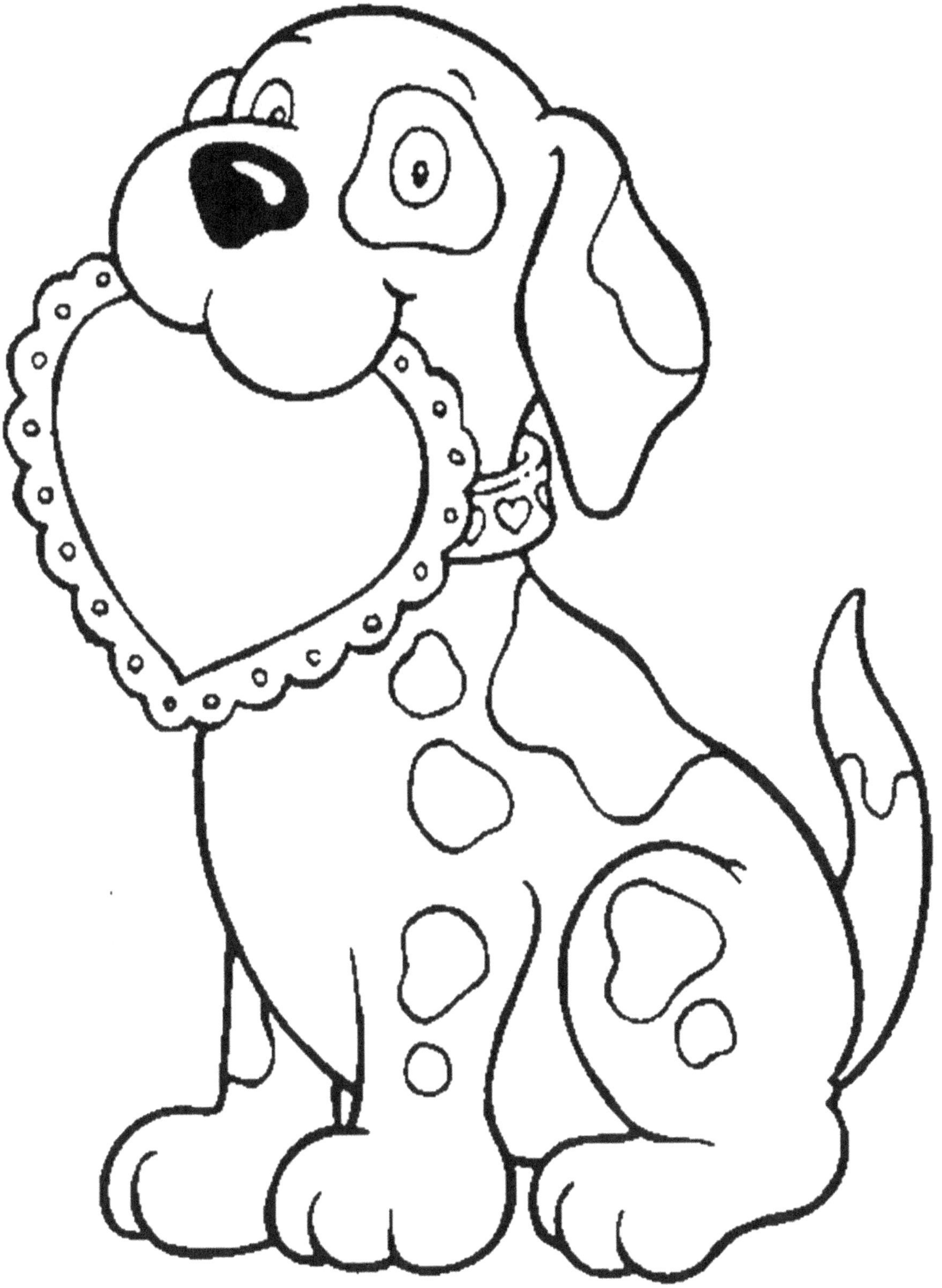

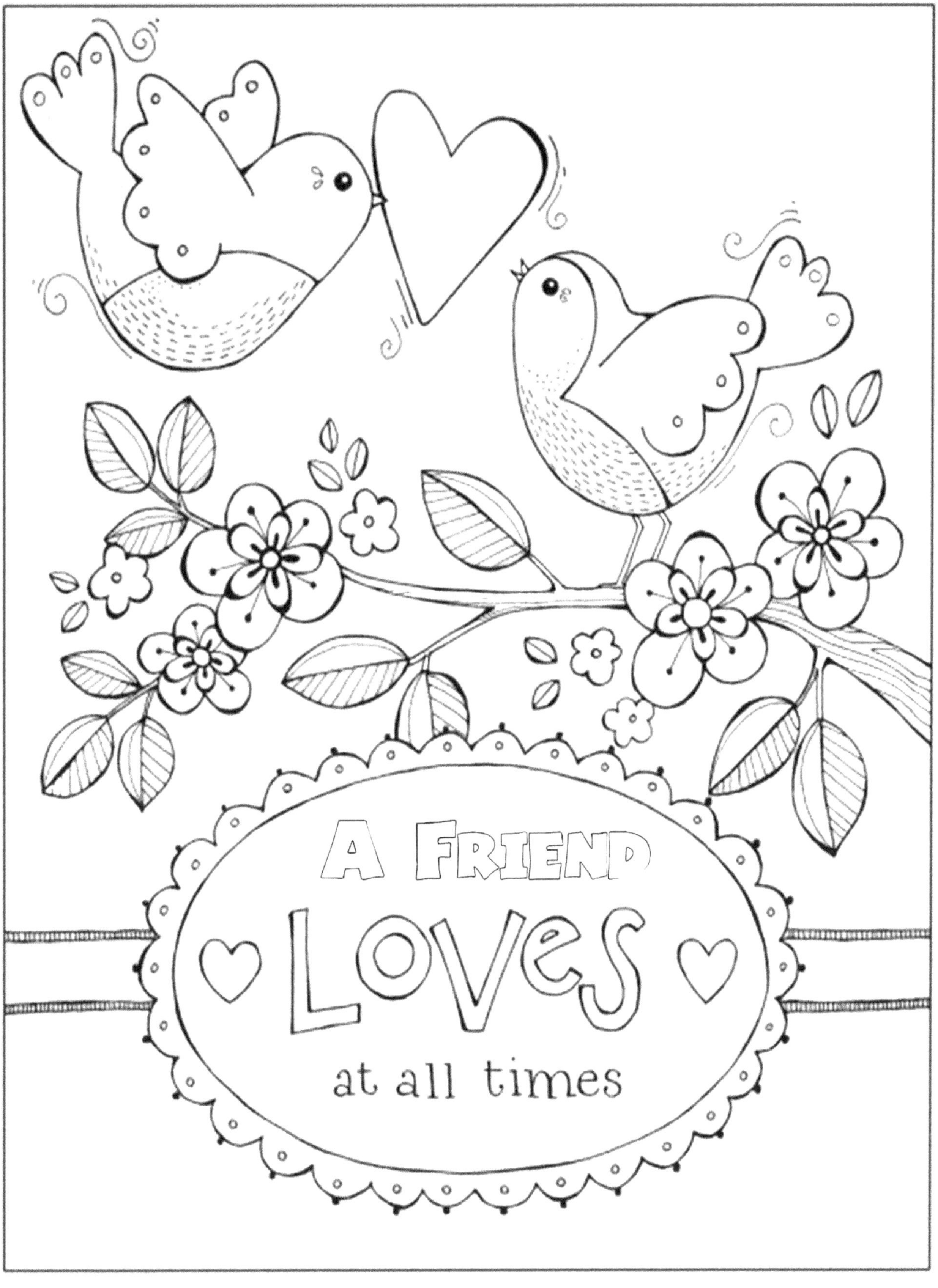
A FRIEND
LOVES
at all times

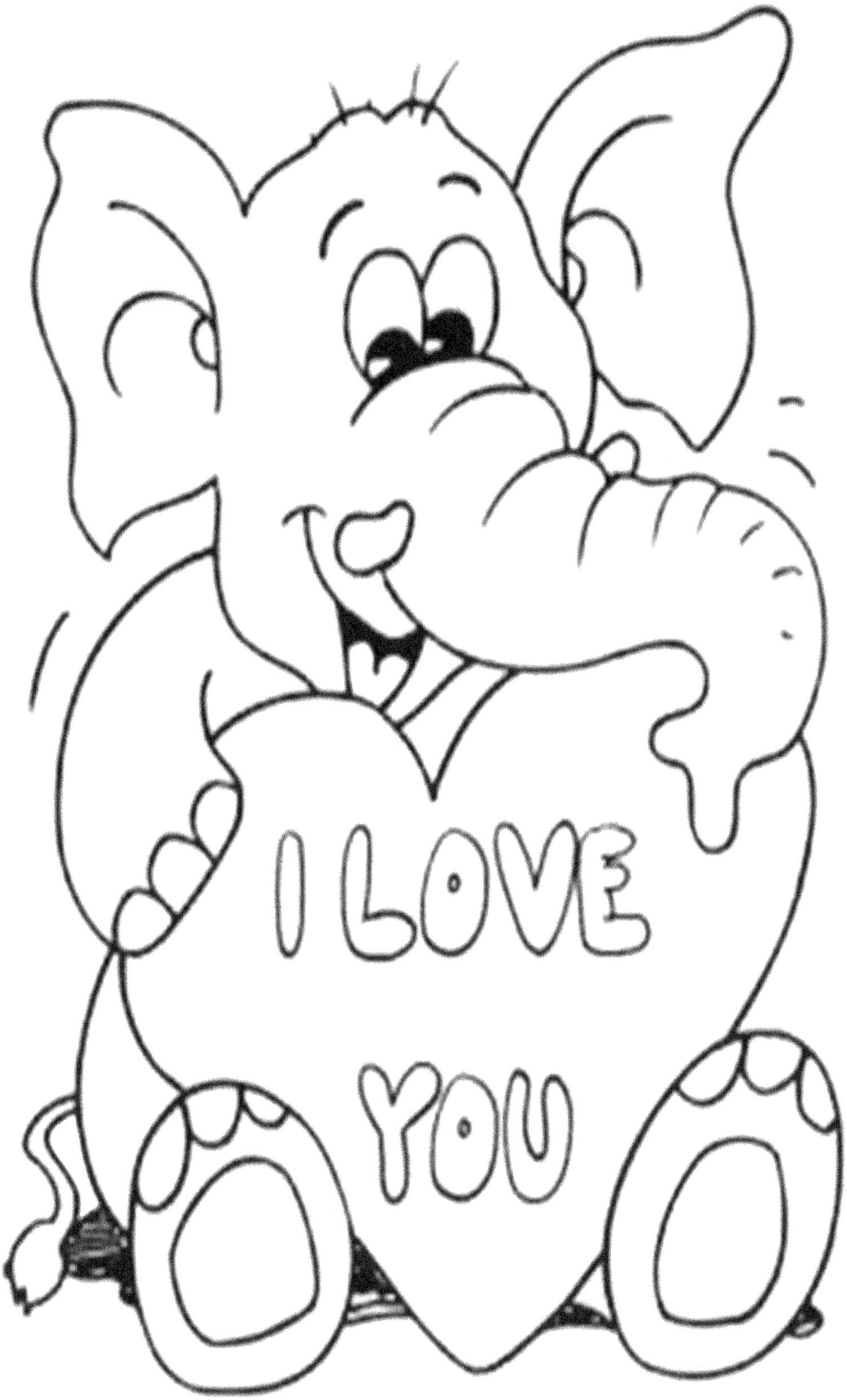
I LOVE
YOU

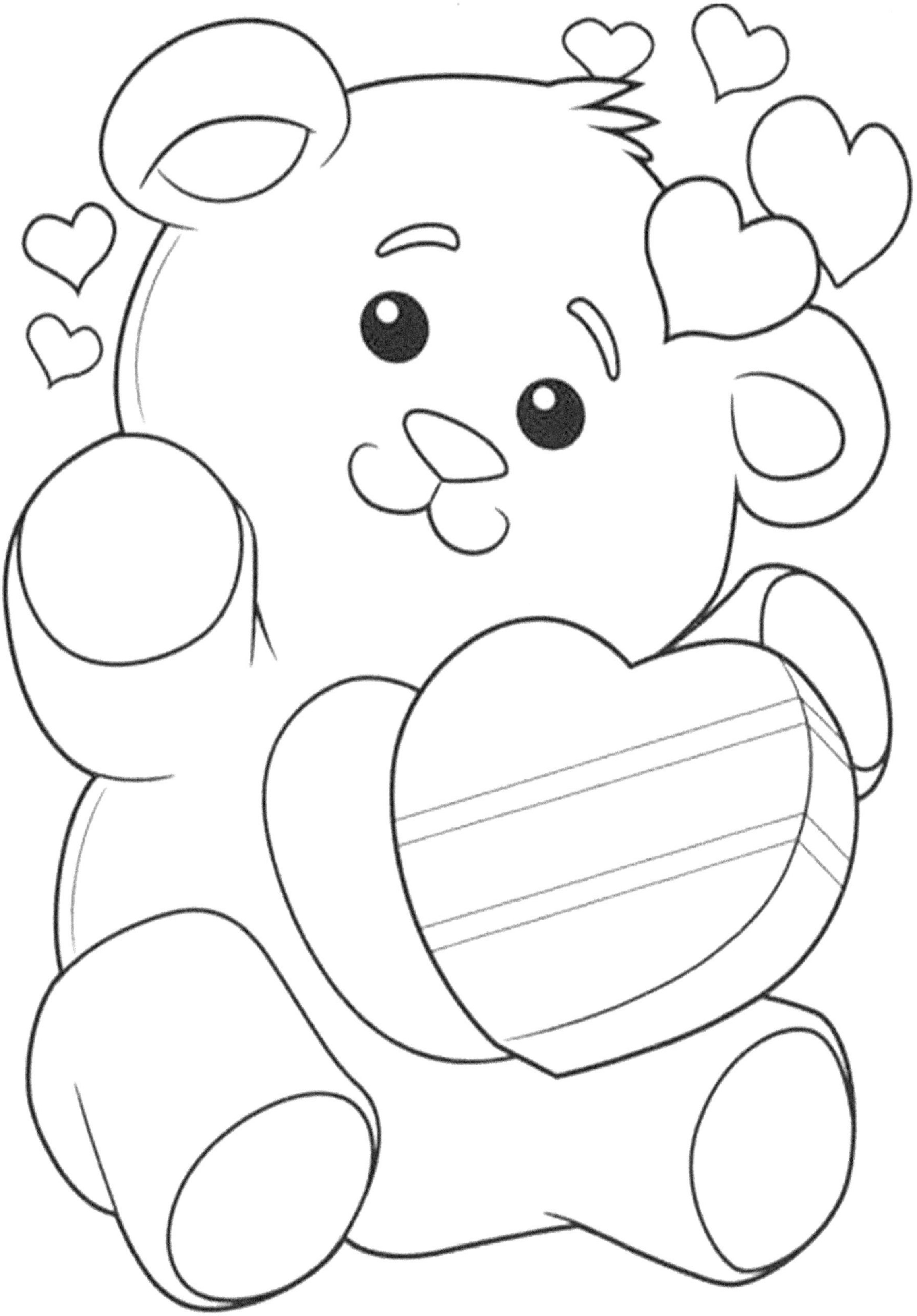

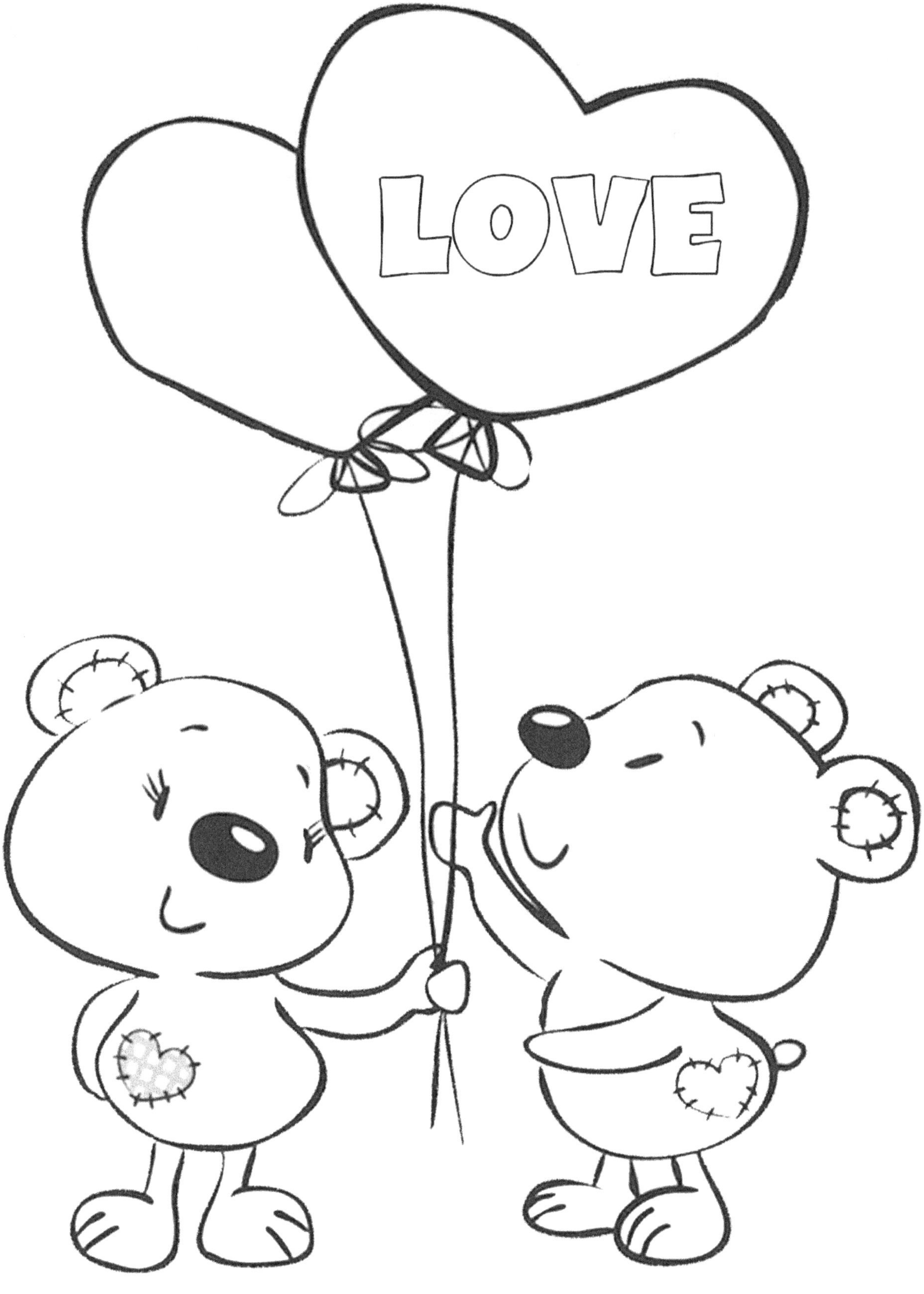
LOVE

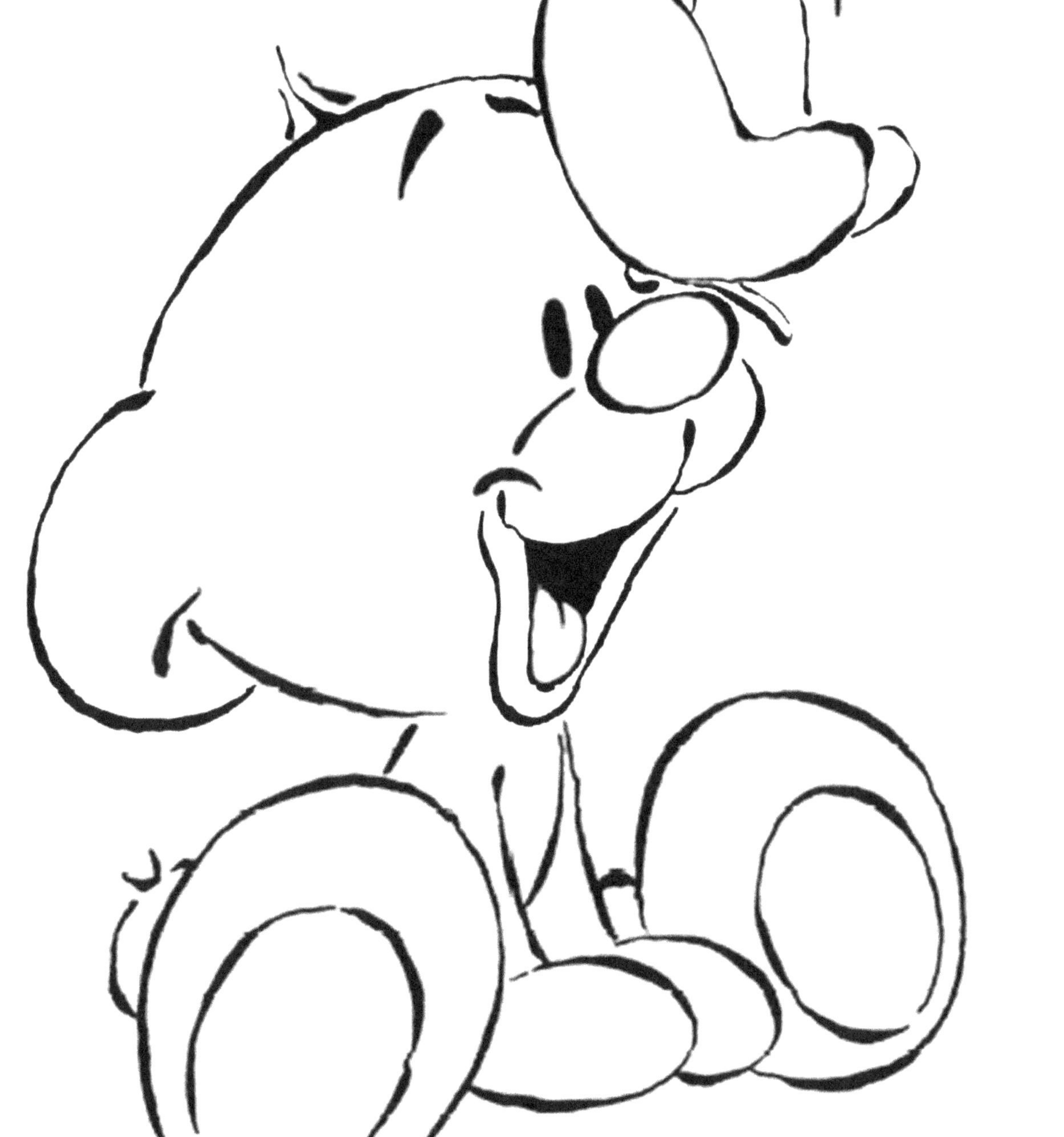
LOVE

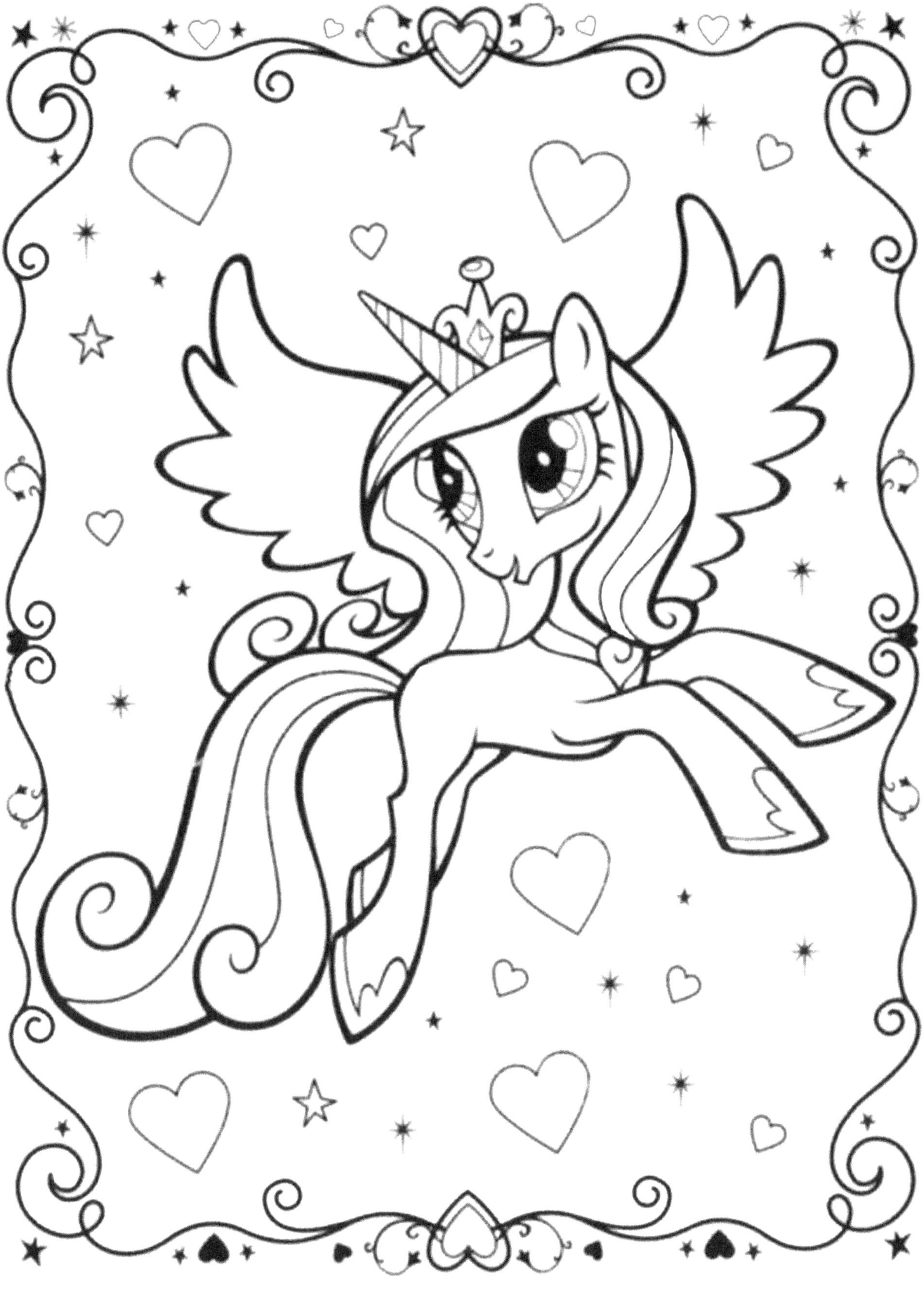

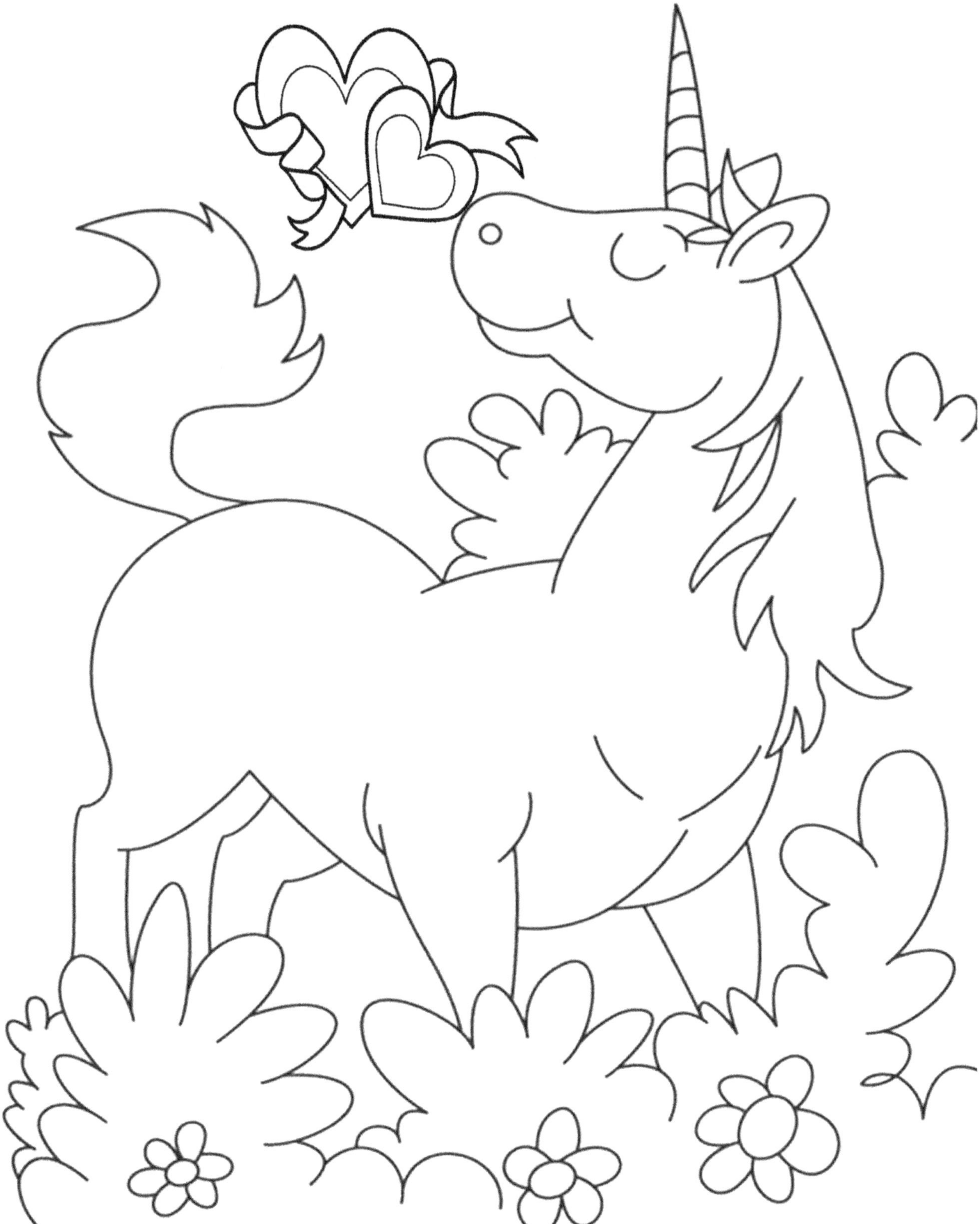

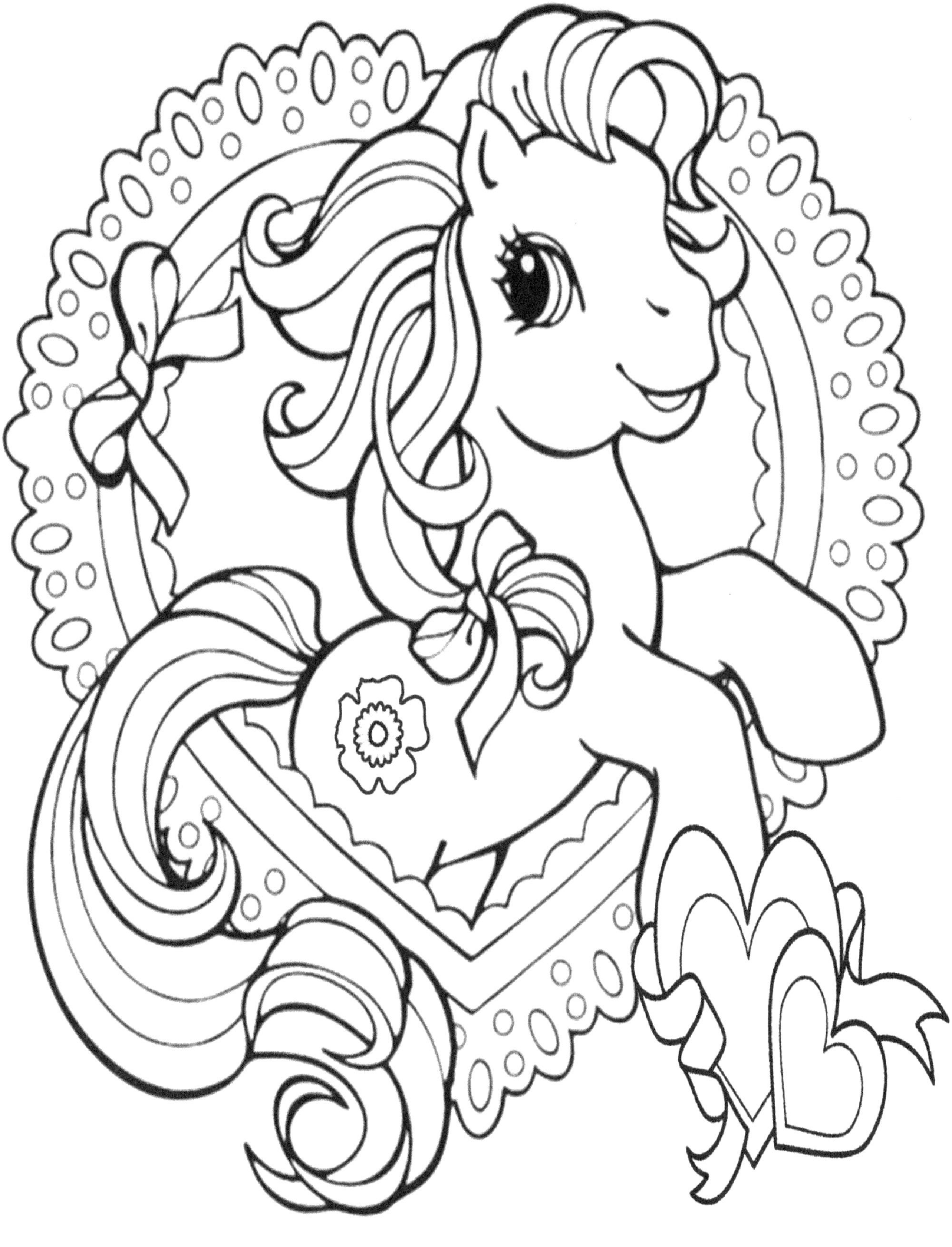

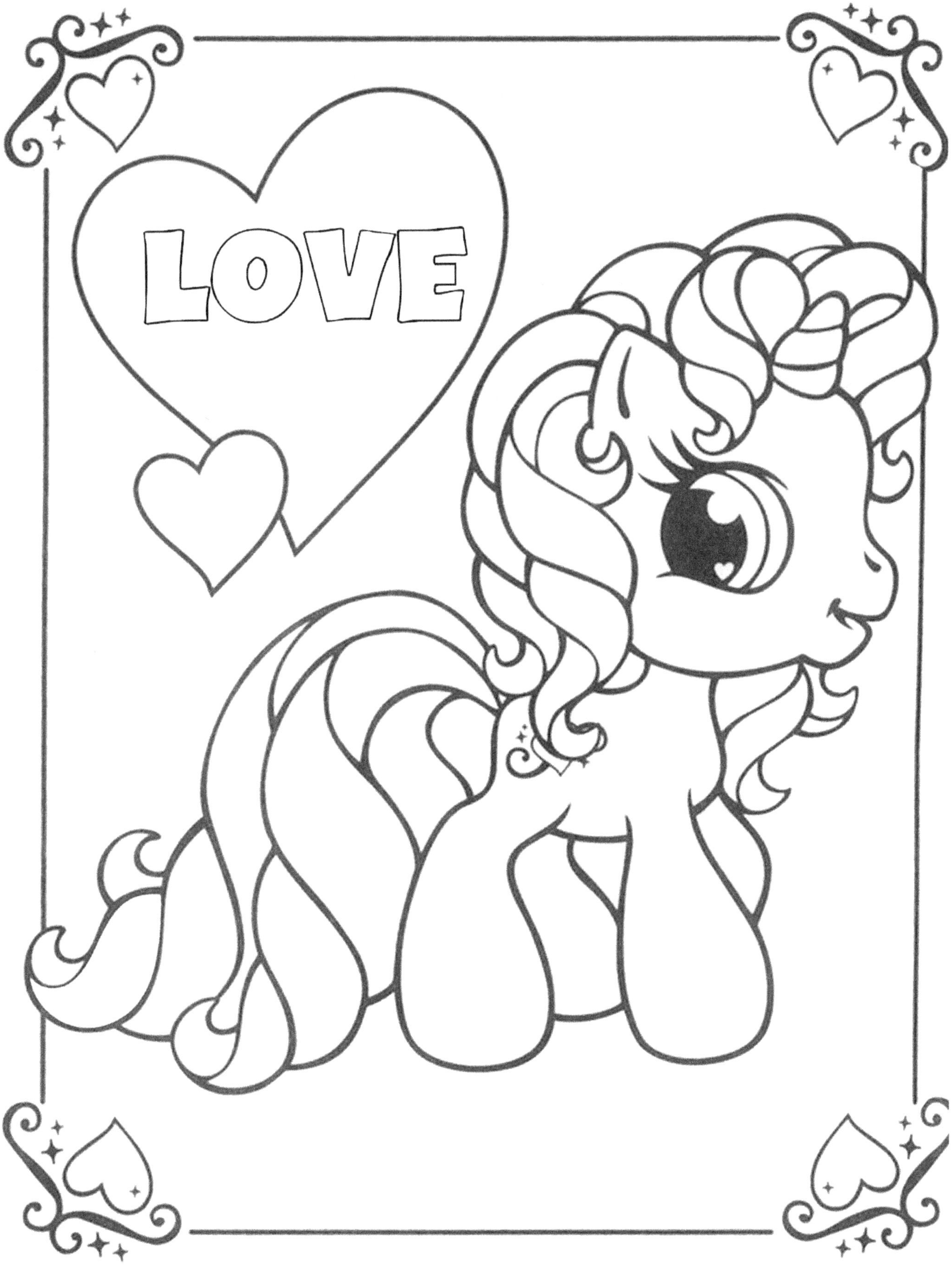
LOVE

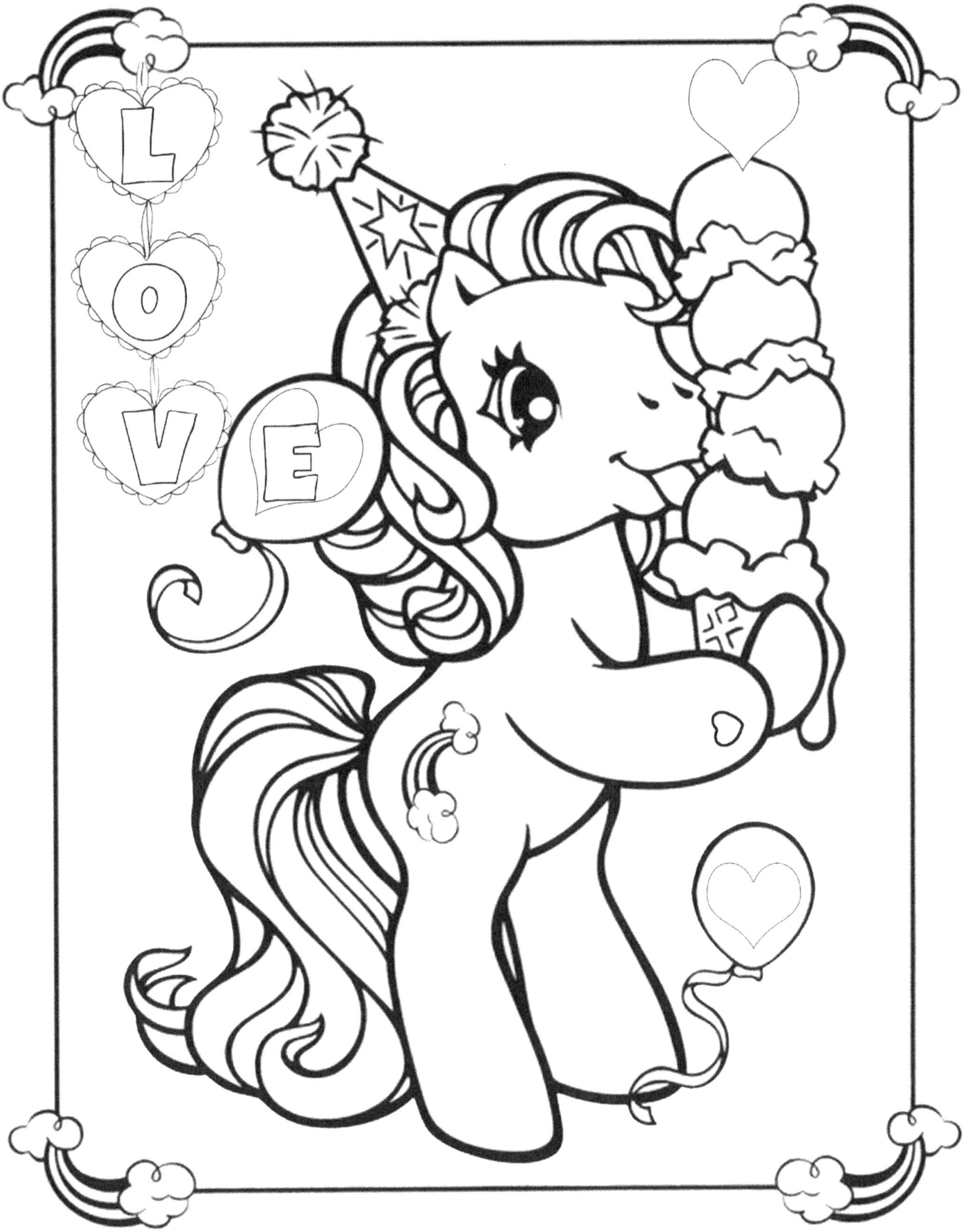
L
O
V
E

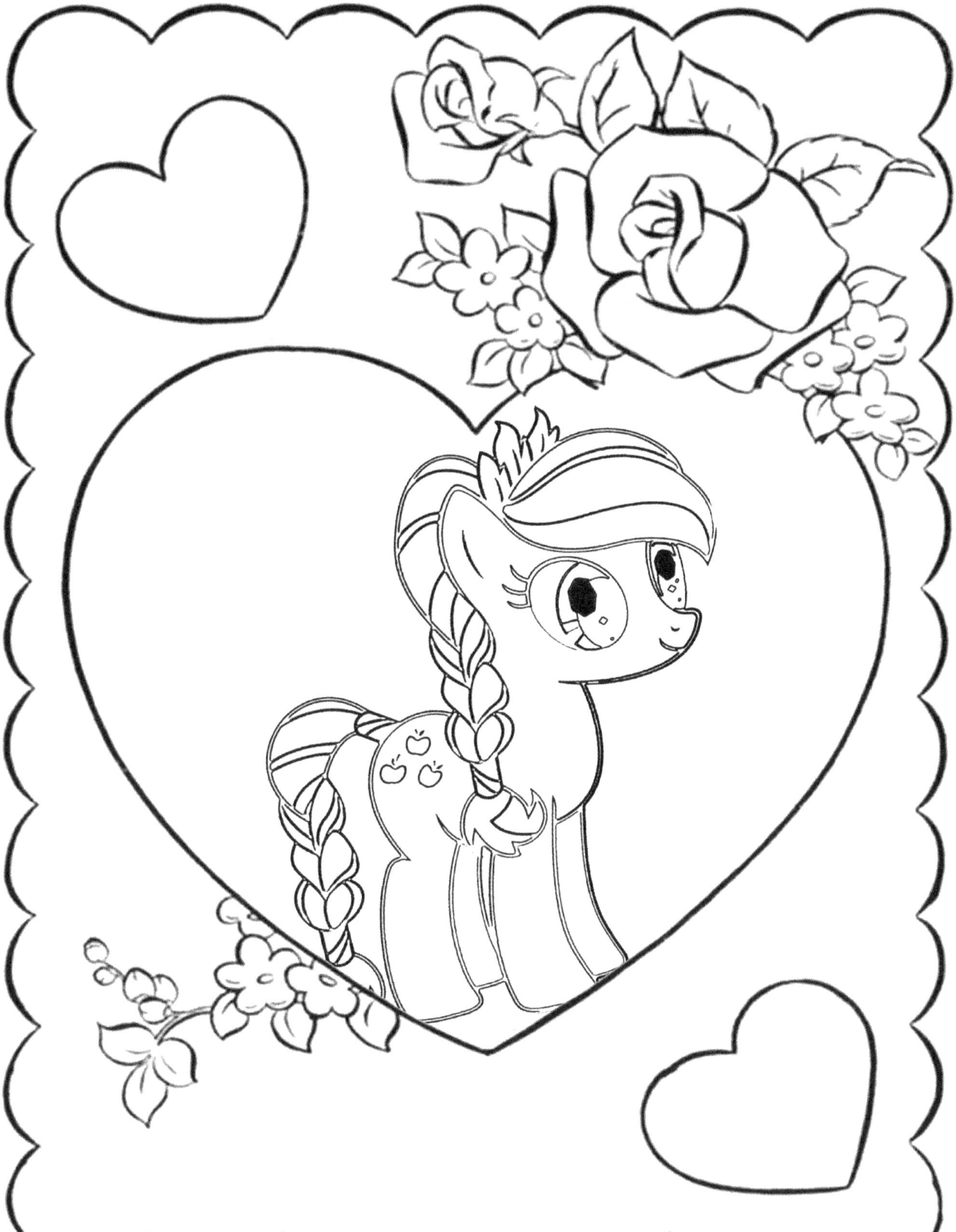

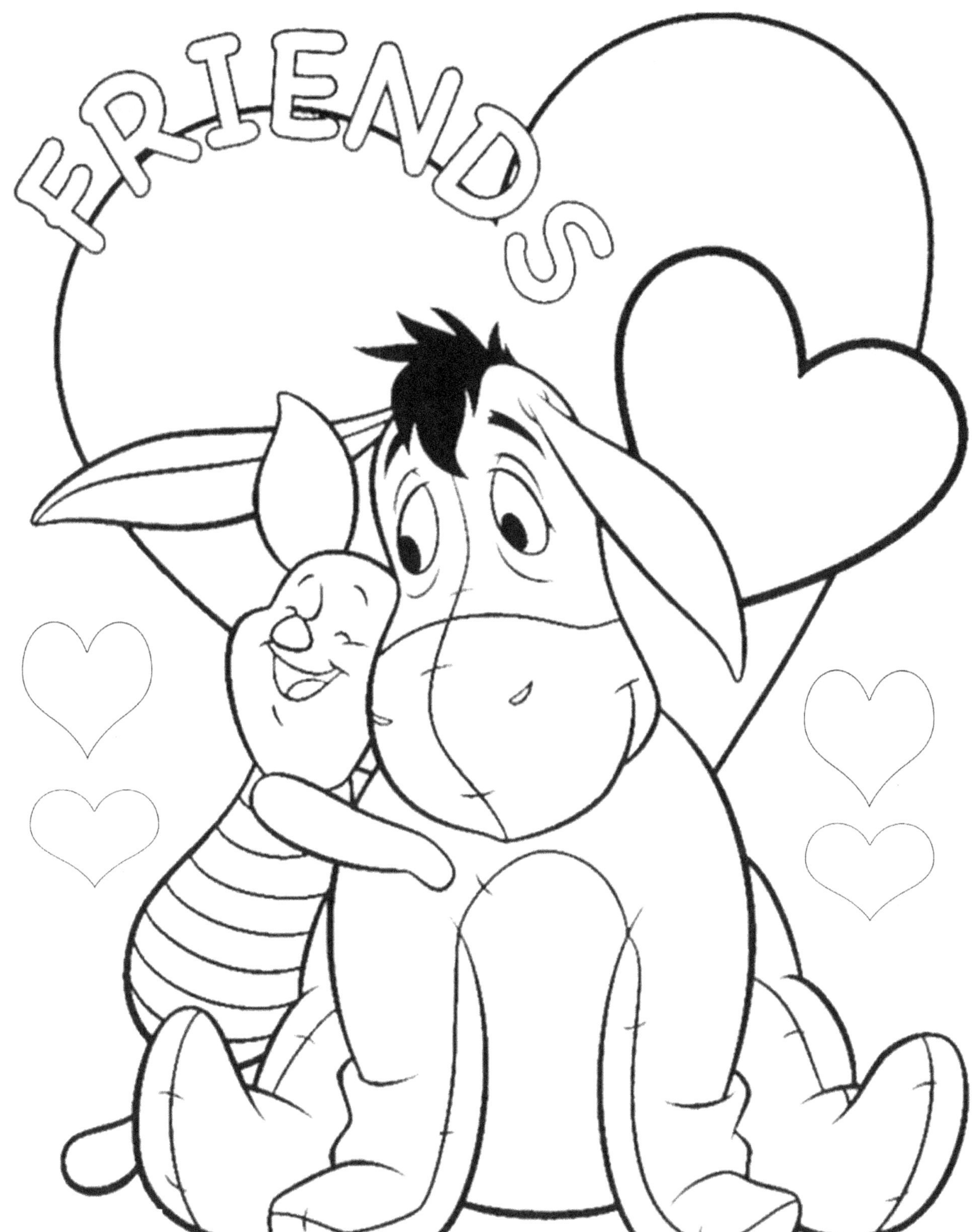
FRIENDS

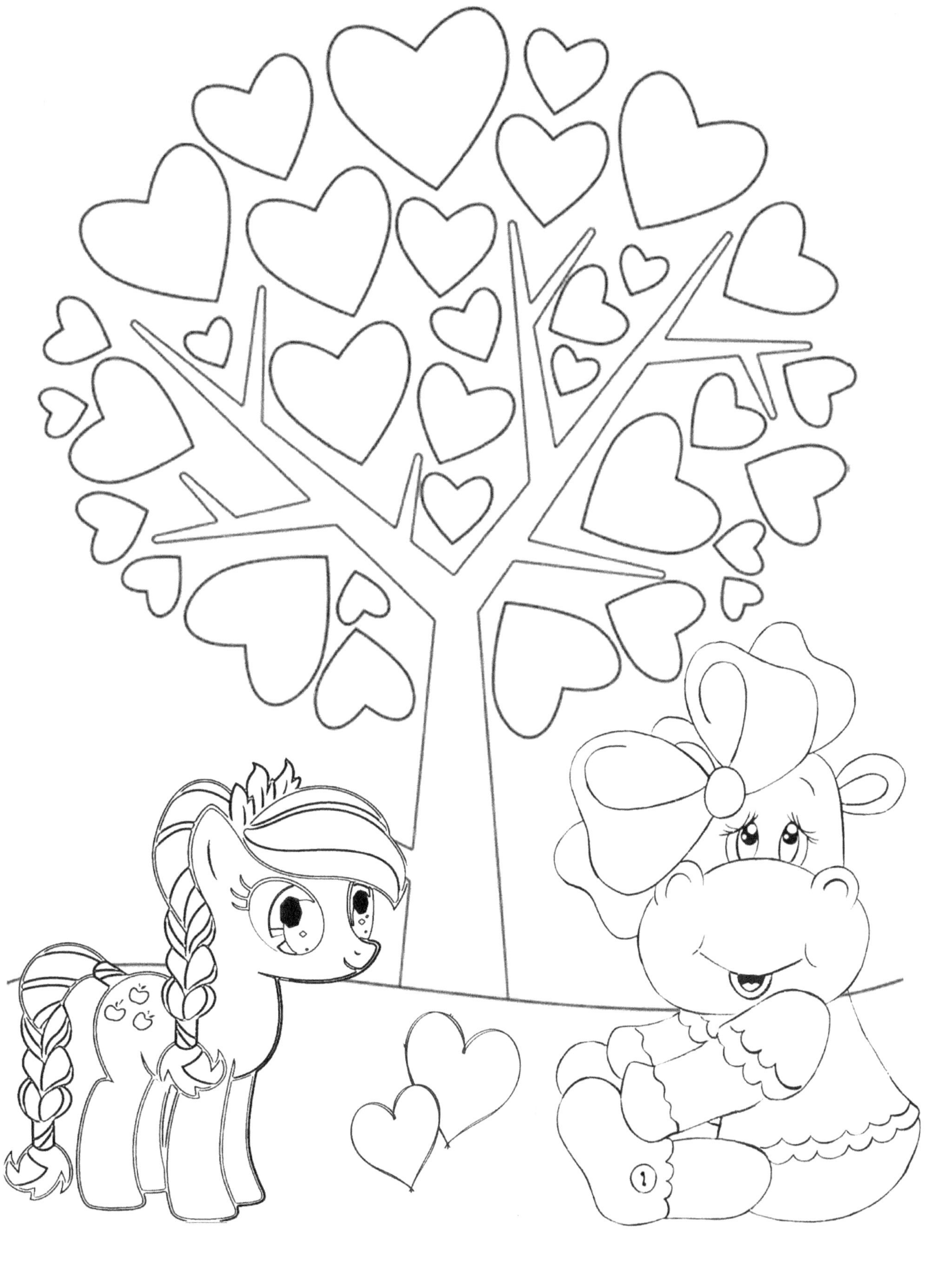

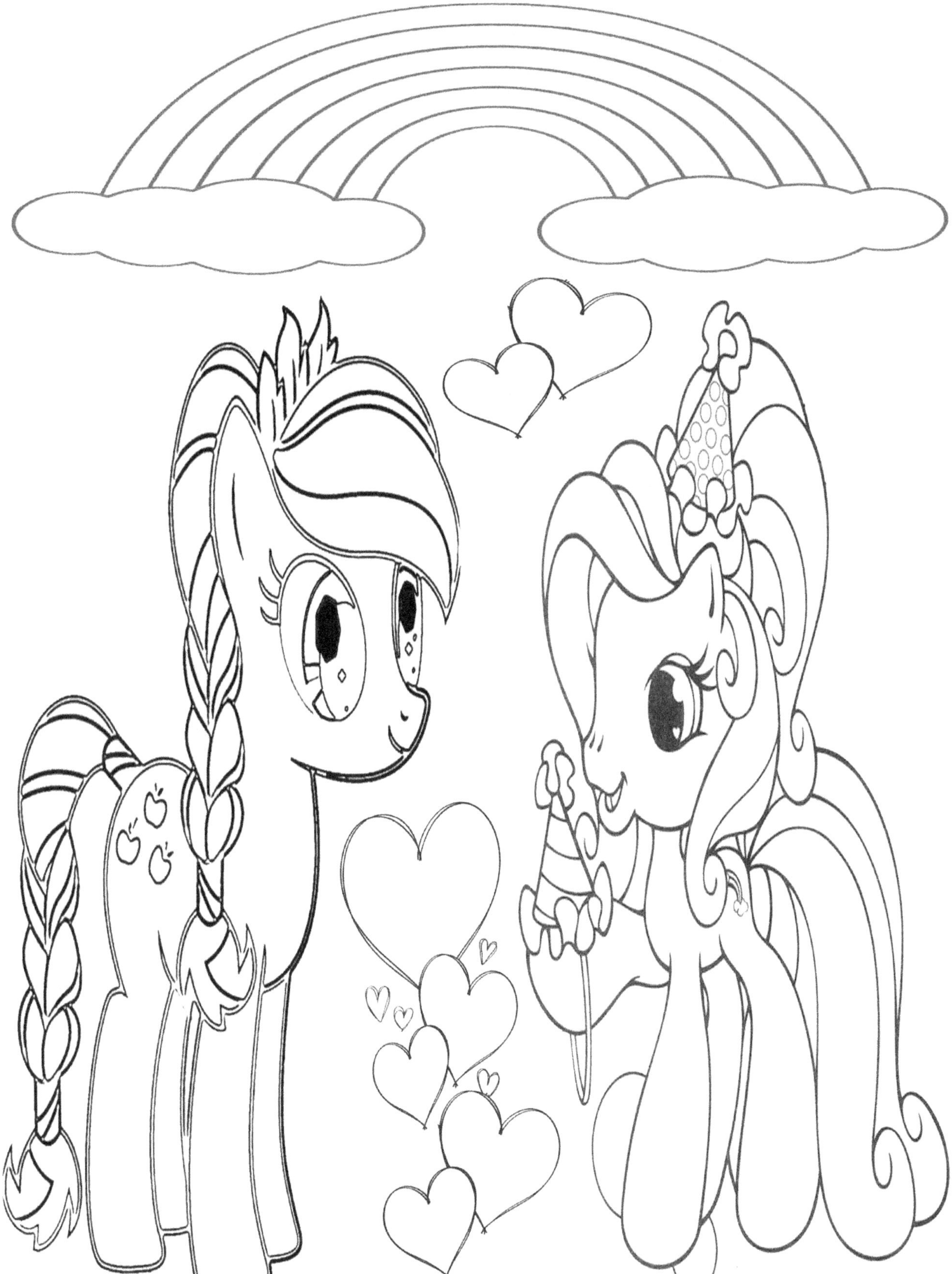

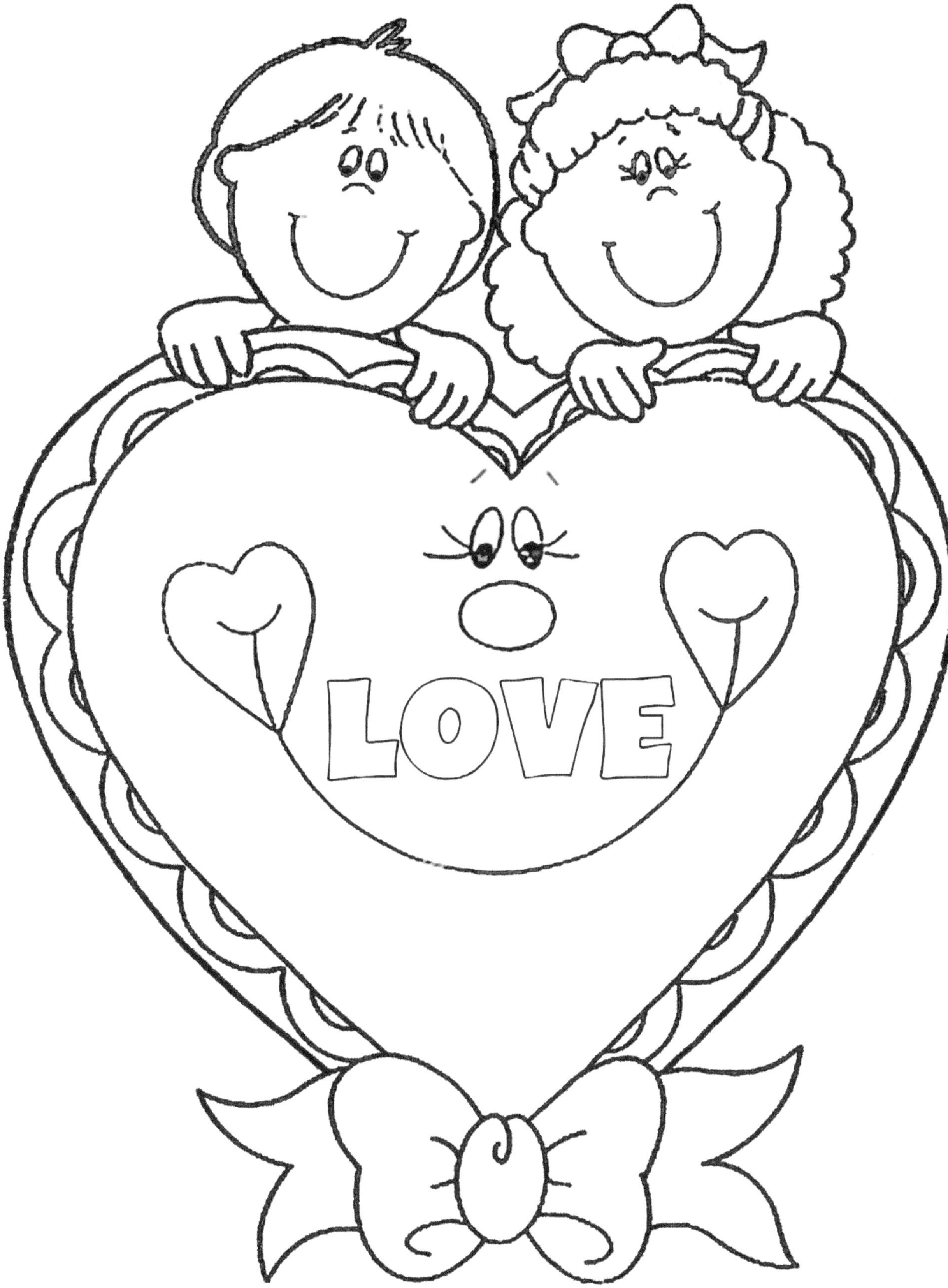
LOVE

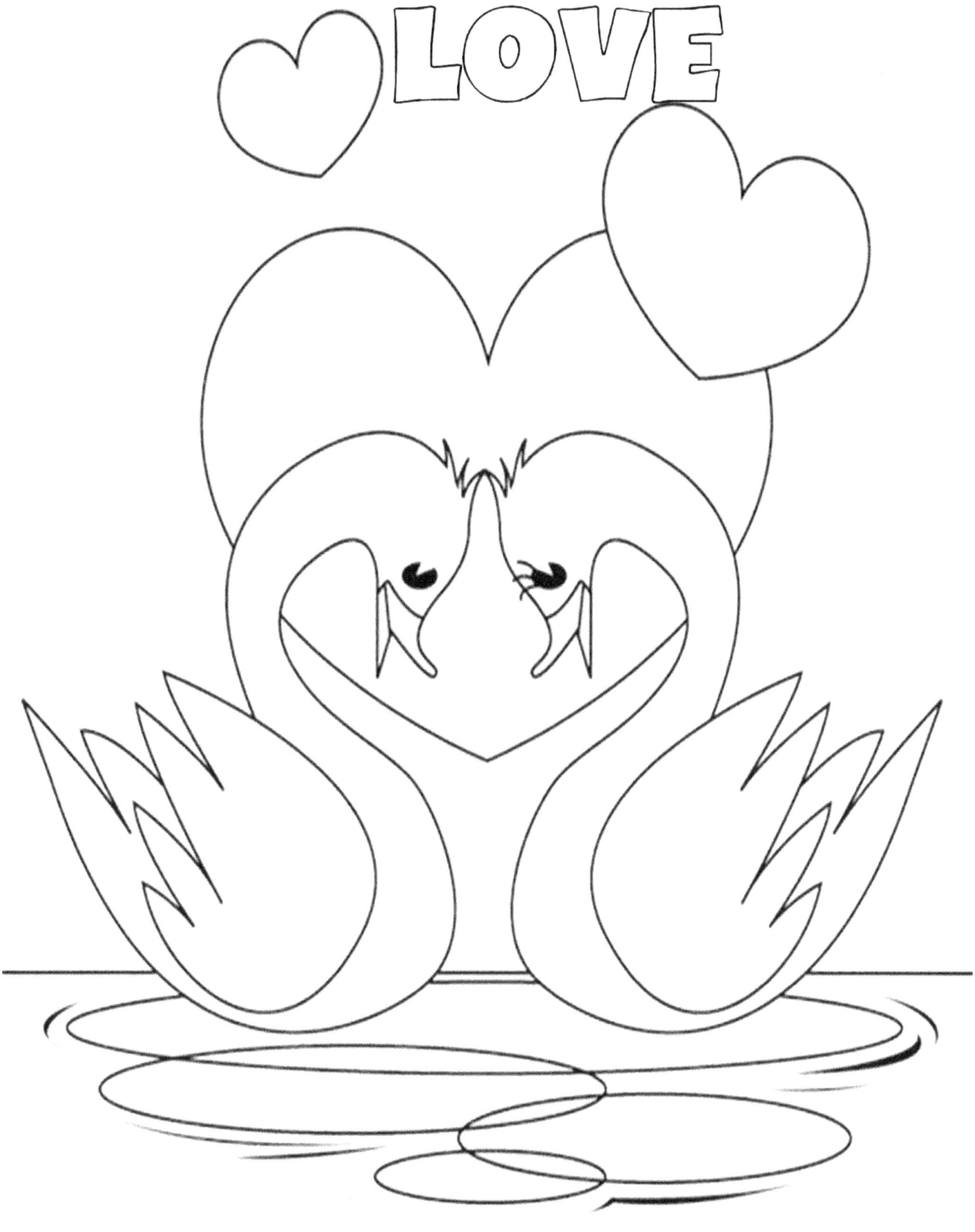
LOVE

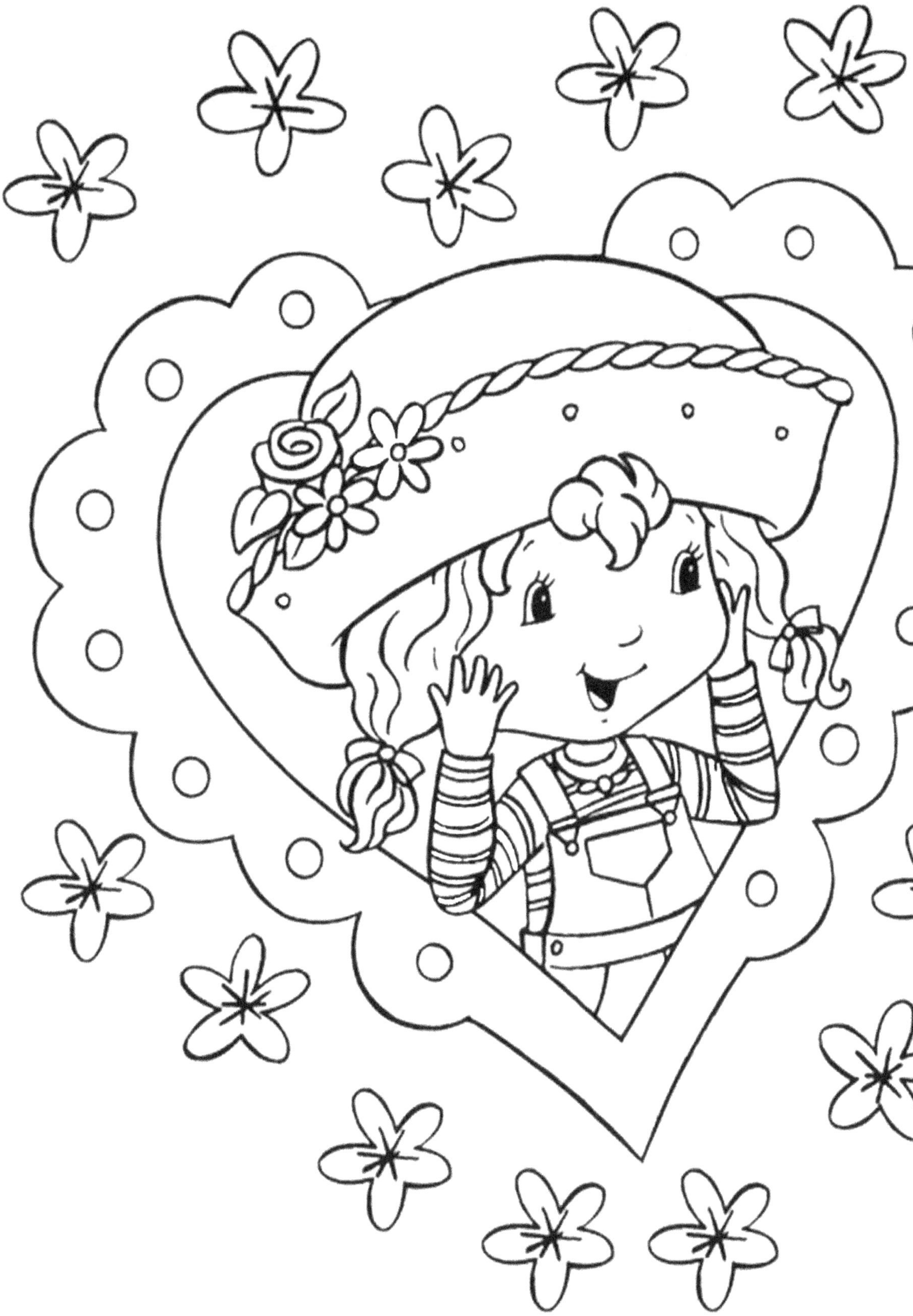

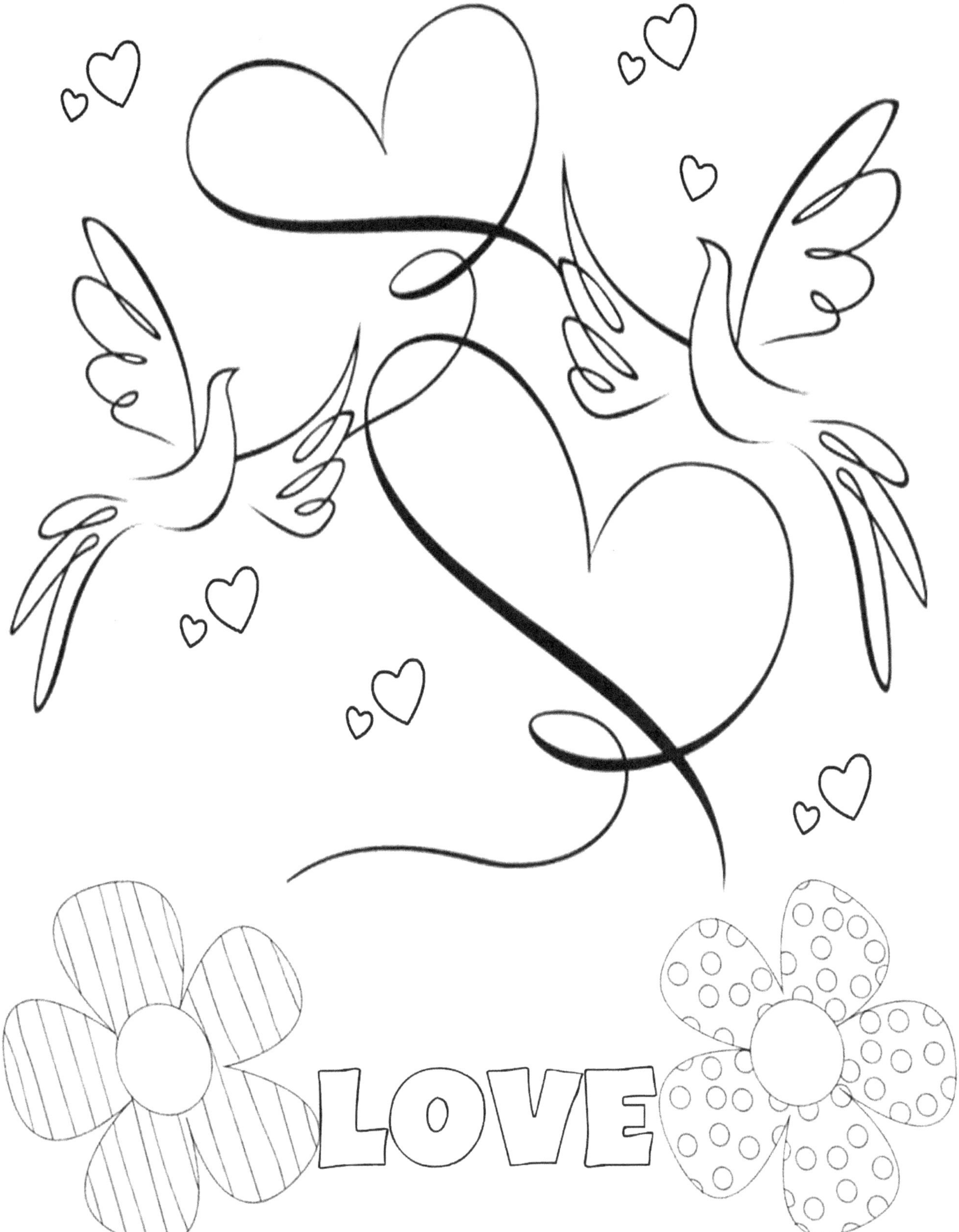
LOVE

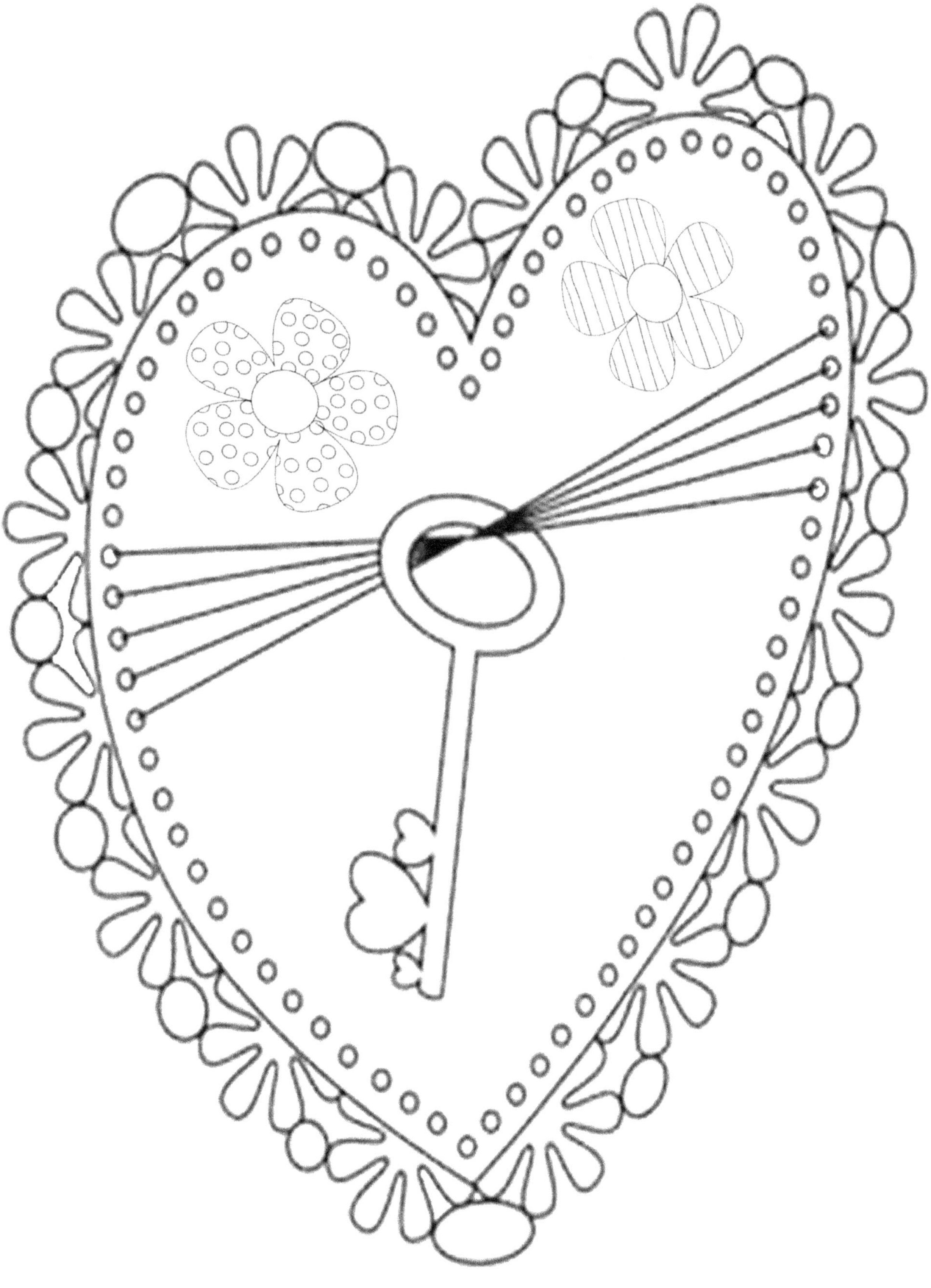

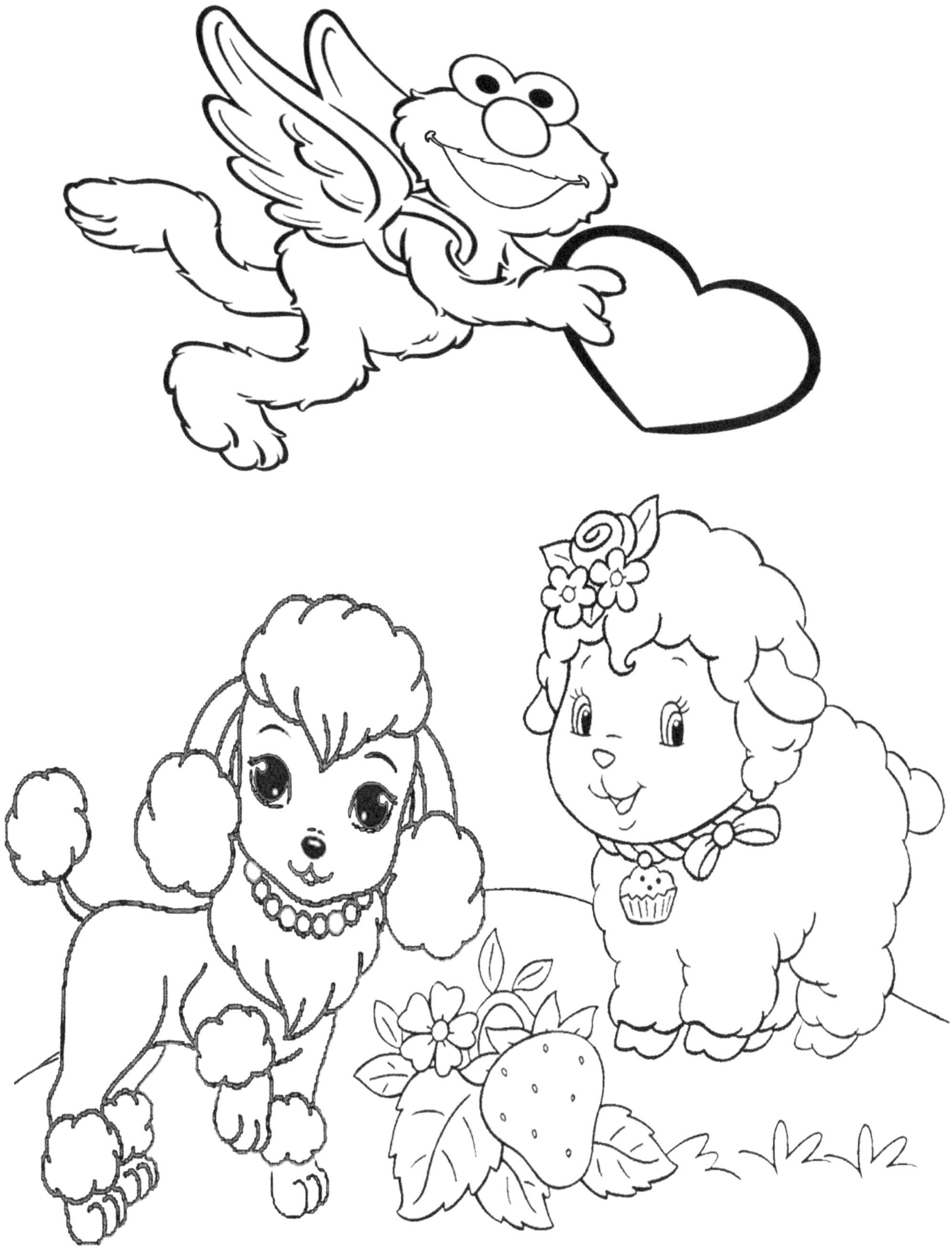

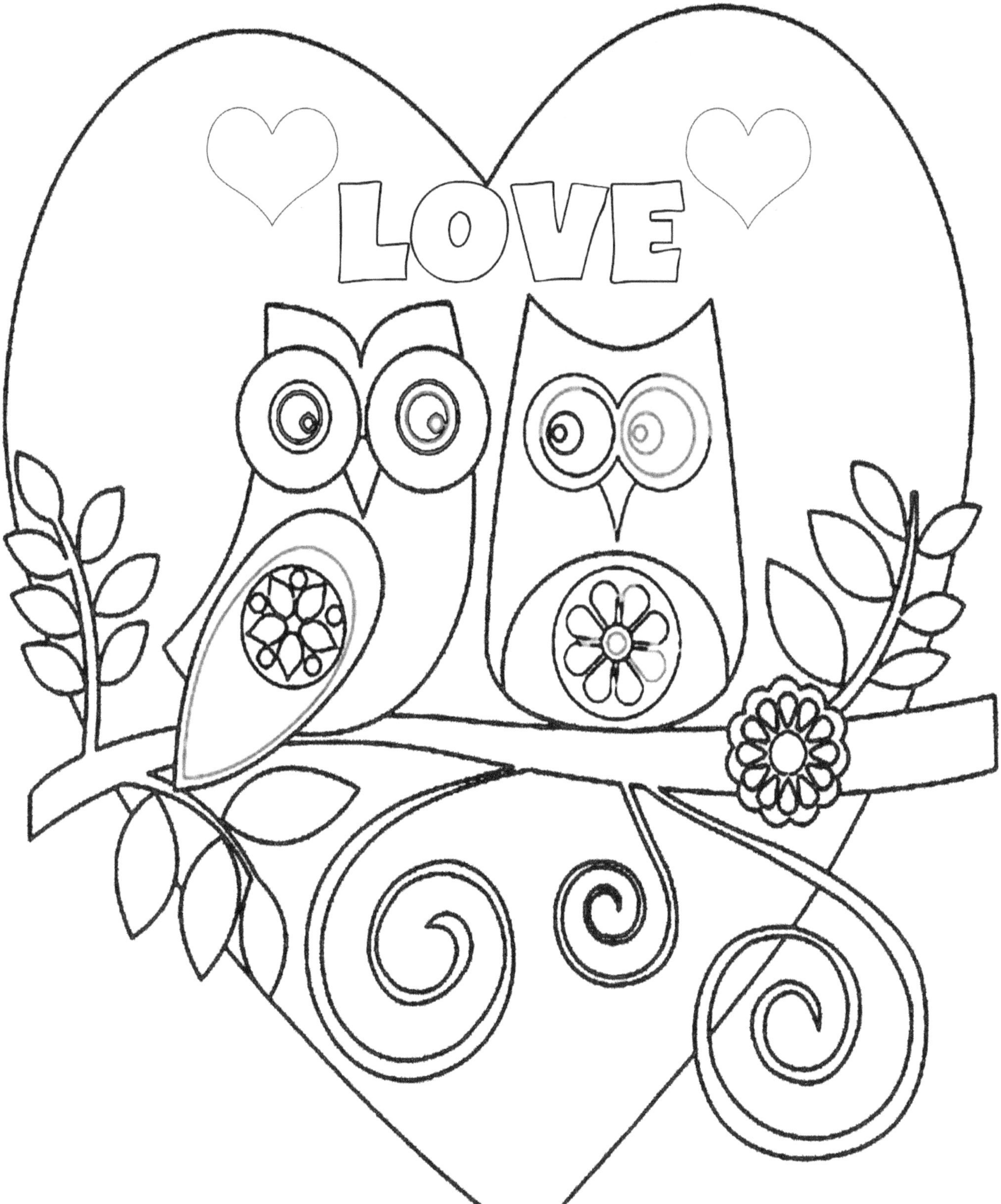
LOVE

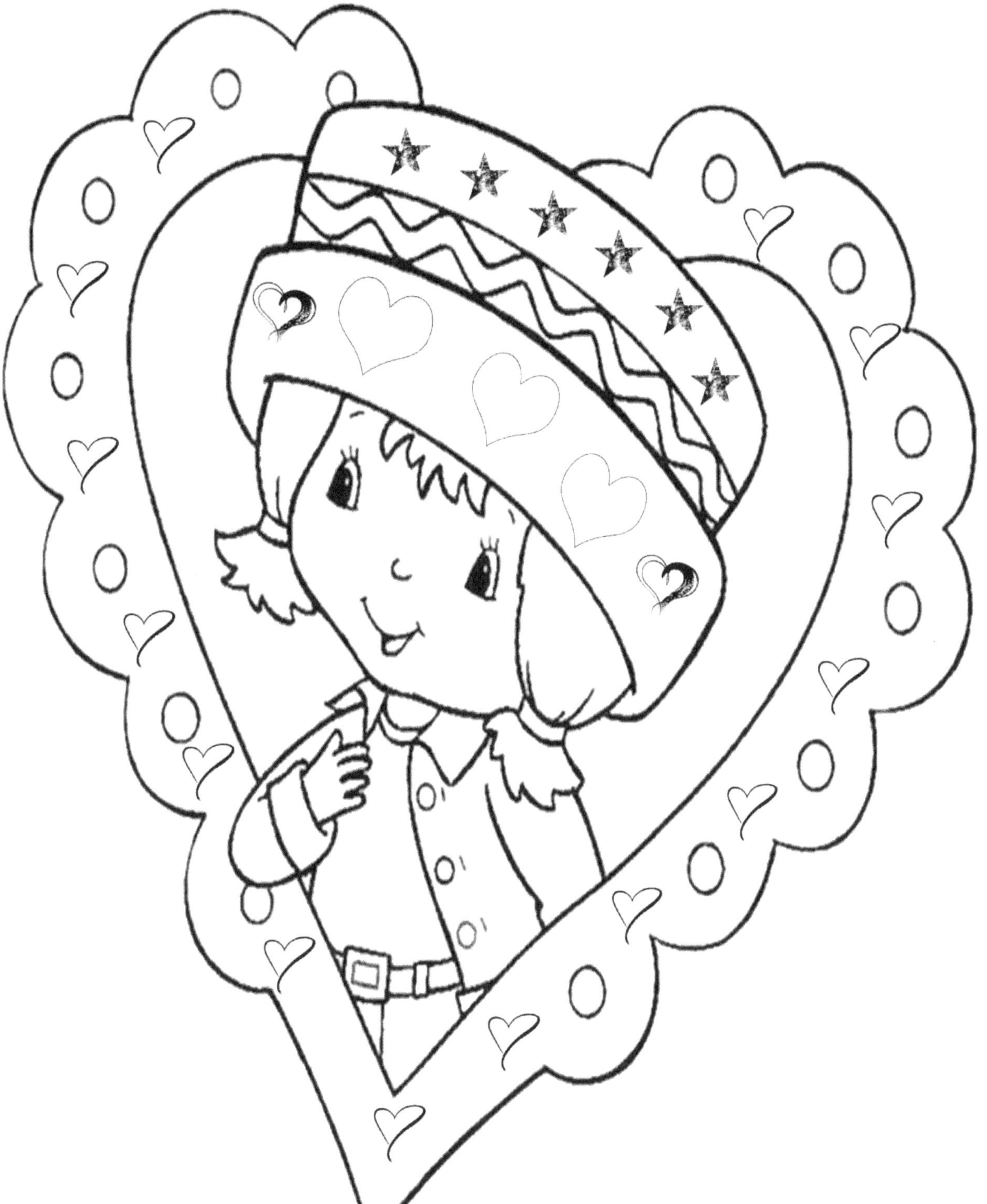

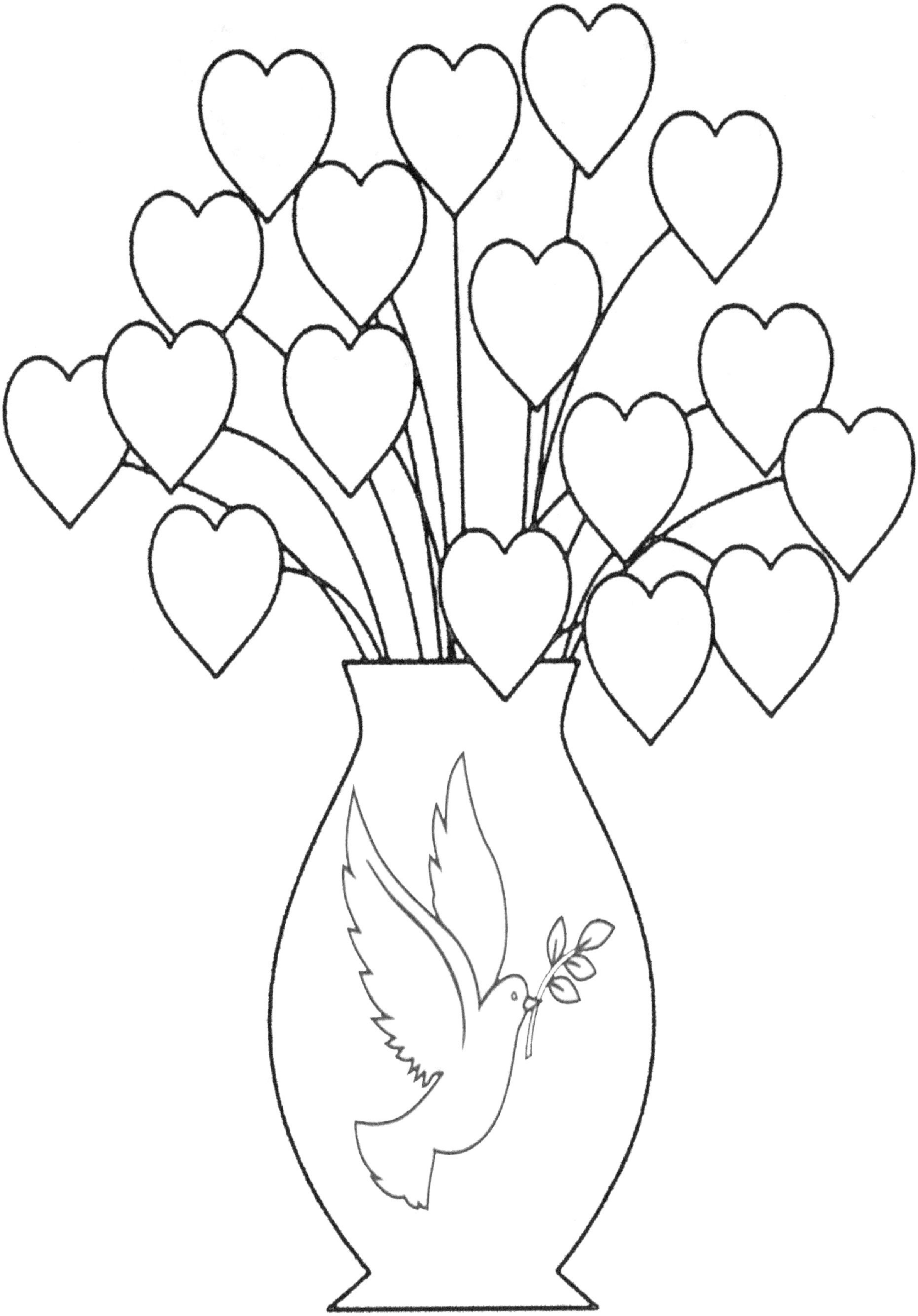

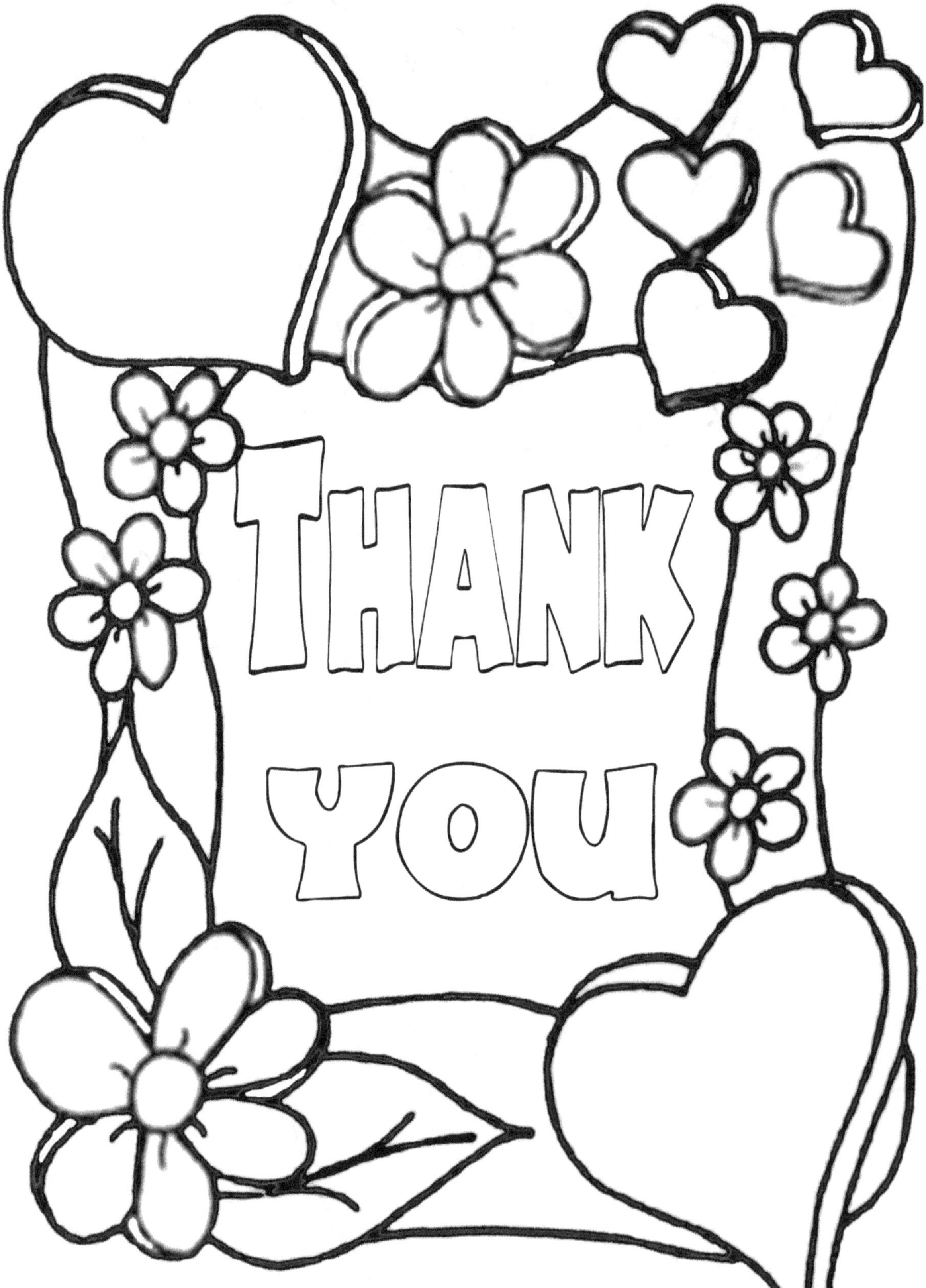
THANK
YOU

www.ingramcontent.com/pod-product-compliance
Lightning Source LLC
Chambersburg PA
CBHW081614220526
45468CB00010B/2874
9781981764754